Twilight II

The Ultimate Screensaver for Your Apple IIGS

Jim R. Maricondo

&

Antoine Vignau

Produced by:
Brian Wiser & Bill Martens

 Apple PugetSound Program Library Exchange

Twilight II: *The Ultimate Screensaver for Your Apple IIGS*

ISBN: 978-1-387-81920-1   2nd Edition

ACKNOWLEDGEMENTS

Twilight II is a trademark of Apple Pugetsound Program Library Exchange (A.P.P.L.E.)

Twilight II was originally published by DigiSoft Innovations in 1990-1993.

Twilight II 1.0 & 2.0 Programming: Jim R. Maricondo

Some modules contain material from the Orca/C Run-Time Libraries, copyright © 1987-1989 Byte Works, Inc. and used with permission.

The Cover, Logo and Book were designed by Brian Wiser.

PRODUCTION

Brian Wiser   → Cover, Logo, Mountains Photo, Design, Layout, Editing
Bill Martens   → Scanning, Proofreading, Screenshots, Disk Updates
Antoine Vignau → IPC documentation, Proofreading, Restoration Programming
Jim Maricondo   → Screenshots, Disk Updates, Programming

DISCLAIMER

About Jim R. Maricondo

Jim R. Maricondo got his first computer, an Apple IIGS, in 1987 after falling in love with the Apple II in school. After teaching himself AppleSoft BASIC he desired to write IIGS applications. However, he did not like Pascal and could not find a book teaching C for the IIGS, so he decided to start with 65816 assembly. He started out reading *Computist* and cracking a few copy-protected games, but desired to write something himself.

Around 1991, he met another teenager online, Jonas Stich, and together they wrote the original *Twilight* screensaver, inspired by *After Dark* on the Mac. There was no Apple IIGS screensaver available at the time, so this was a big market opportunity. (A little while later, he also banded together with a few other teenagers he met online to create DYA, the Digital Youth Alliance, with the goal of writing demos and software for the IIGS. DYA had one main release, a self-booting slideshow for the IIGS. The first Twilight was $10 shareware and Jonas and Jim agreed to split the revenue (from probably around 100-150 paying users in total). Unfortunately, after about a year Jonas went off to college and the checks from Jonas, who collected the money, stopped coming in. Meanwhile, it became apparent there were a lot of bugs and areas for improvement.

Jim decided to rewrite the app himself, naming it "Twilight II" and sought to have it published commercially. But this was 1992 right when the bottom was falling out of the Apple II market. So, he decided to publish it himself, founding DigiSoft Innovations in the process. Matt Keller and Derek Young from DYA helped contribute art and effects modules. Critically, Jim met James C. Smith online and James went on to author the most famous modules such as Fractal Mountains, Fireworks, SLED (Super LED Sign). To write the manual, Jim borrowed a Mac Classic from James which was shipped from Wisconsin to Connecticut so that he could use the booklet making plug-in module for *Aldus PageMaker*, and had it printed at a neighborhood print shop that he actually toured originally in preschool.

Originally 1,000 copies of the manual were produced, but eventually a second printing was required. Jim sold many copies directly, at trade fairs (including its [beta] debut at Apple Expo East 1992, and later Apple Expo West in April 1993), and through distributors like Big Red Computer Club, offering "competitive upgrades" from *Signature*, the only real competition, and discounts for user groups and referrals from groups like Shareware Solutions. It is estimated that around 1400 copies were sold in total, to the last batch of loyal Apple II diehards. ("II Infinitum!")

Some other tidbits: Jim was always concerned about performance, that having *Twilight II* running in the background would not slow down the speed of the computer too much. Of course, when a screen saver is running, the original program stops (except for the background mode, which just dims the screen but lets the original program continue running, by changing the color palettes.) By far, the most popular animation on *After Dark* on the Mac was the Flying Toasters. Jim didn't want to publish an outright copy of it, but eventually Nathan Mates ported the graphics with *PhotoShop* and created a module called Toast (which like the YouDrawIt module, allows you to draw frames in a template which is later animated.)

Unfortunately, in 1994 like Jonas before, Jim also went off to college and *Twilight II* development ground to a halt. Jim started an upgrade to *Twilight II* but unfortunately never managed to finish it. Nathan Mates offered to complete it, so Jim provided him the source and later forgot about it. The source of the Nathan Mates version is probably lost to history. In the late 2010s, Bill Martens got Jim to dig up the version 2.0 beta source from his old hard drive so it could be archived and re-released in 2020. Special thanks to Bill Martens, Brian Wiser, and of course Antoine Vignau for this release!

After *Twilight II*, Jim worked as a software engineer writing Internet security software, financial trading systems, and eventually Web apps, in Silicon Valley in Japan, before eventually transitioning to a career in business development and technology evangelism. He currently resides in Japan and is passionate about blockchain and cryptocurrency. Some of Jim's projects are available at: https://tezmania.jp and https://digisoft.callapple.org

About Antoine Vignau

Antoine Vignau discovered the Apple II at the age of 10. After months of discoveries, he wrote his first assembly language routines. Later on, he became interested in copy protection schemes. In 1992, he founded Brutal Deluxe Software with Olivier Zardini. They have released numerous top-notch programs for the Apple II and IIGS, encompassing entertainment, utilities, and software preservation. Noteworthy titles include *LemminGS* and *The Tinies*.

Antoine is also the curator of the Apple II Documentation Project which aims to preserve all hardware-related items for the Apple II computers. And, he has made contributions to numerous projects by recovering, compiling, and enhancing legacy source code for key programs such as *Twilight II*, *DOS 4.4*, *GS/OS System 6*, *GBBS*, and *Sword of Sodan*. Today, Antoine works in IT where he has held different positions in large industrial companies. Read more about Brutal Deluxe and Antoine's archival projects at: https://www.brutaldeluxe.fr

About the Producers

Brian Wiser

Brian Wiser is a producer of books, films, games, and events, as well as a long-time consultant, enthusiast and historian of Apple, the Apple II and Macintosh. Steve Wozniak and Steve Jobs, as well as *Creative Computing*, *Nibble*, *InCider*, and *A+* magazines were early influences.

Brian designed, edited, and co-produced dozens of books including: *Nibble Viewpoints: Business Insights From The Computing Revolution*, *Cyber Jack: The Adventures of Robert Clardy and Synergistic Software*, *Synergistic Software: The Early Games*, *The Colossal Computer Cartoon Book: Enhanced Edition*, *All About Applesoft: Enhanced Edition*, *Graphically Speaking: Enhanced Edition*, *What's Where in the Apple: Enhanced Edition*, and *The WOZPAK: Special Edition* – an important Apple II historical book with Steve Wozniak's restored original, technical handwritten notes. Brian is also the author of *The Etch-a-Sketch and Other Fun Programs*.

He passionately preserves and archives all facets of Apple's history, and noteworthy companies such as Beagle Bros and Applied Engineering, featured on AppleArchives.com. His writing, interviews and books are featured on the technology news site CallApple.org and in *Call-A.P.P.L.E.* magazine that he co-produces as an A.P.P.L.E. board member. Brian also co-produced the retro iOS game *Structris*.

In 2005, Brian was cast as an extra in Joss Whedon's movie *Serenity*, leading him to being a producer and director for the documentary film *Done The Impossible: The Fans' Tale of Firefly & Serenity*. He brought some of the *Firefly* cast aboard his Browncoat Cruise and recruited several of the *Firefly* cast to appear in a film for charity. Throughout these experiences, he develops close personal relationships with many actors, authors, and computer industry luminaries. Brian speaks about his adventures to large audiences at conventions around the country.

Bill Martens

Bill Martens is a systems engineer specializing in office infrastructures and has been programming since 1976. The DEC PDP 11/40 with ASR-33 Teletypes and CRT's were his first computing platforms with his first forays in the Apple world coming with the Apple II computer.

Influences in Bill's computing life came from *Byte* magazine, *Creative Computing* magazine, and *Call-A.P.P.L.E.* magazine as well as his mentors Samuel Perkins, Don Williams, Joff Morgan, and Mike Christensen.

Bill is the author of *ApPilot/W1*, *Beyond Quest*, *The Anatomy of an EAMON*, and multiple EAMon adventure games, as well as a co-producer of many books including *What's Where in the Apple: Enhanced Edition*, *The WOZPAK: Special Edition*, *Nibble Viewpoints: Business Insights From The Computing Revolution*, and co-programmer for the iOS version of the retro game *Structris*. He has written many articles which have appeared in user group newsletters and magazines such as *Call-A.P.P.L.E.*.

Bill worked for Apple Pugetsound Program Library Exchange (A.P.P.L.E.) under Val Golding and Dick Hubert as a data manager and programmer in the 1980s, and is the current president of the A.P.P.L.E. user group established in 1978. He reorganized A.P.P.L.E. and restarted *Call-A.P.P.L.E.* magazine in 2002. He is the production editor for the A.P.P.L.E. website CallApple.org, writes science fiction novels in his spare time, and is a retired semi-pro football player.

CONTENTS

About Twilight II

Starting Out

Reference

Appendices

ABOUT TWILIGHT II

The Ultimate Screen Saver for Your Apple IIGS

Are You Upset?

Are you angered by the way the Apple IIGS has been treated lately? Sick of your friends bragging that they have the better computer? Does seeing *After Dark* on the IBM or Mac make you wonder, "Why can't my Apple IIGS do that?" Do you like dazzling effects that will protect your valuable monitor from becoming useless when the same image is left onscreen for so long that it burned into the glass? Are you tired of dull screen savers that slow you down and interfere with your work, from companies that don't want to upgrade their products? If so, then read on!

Thank you very much for your purchase of *Twilight II*™, the ultimate Apple IIGS screen saver! *Twilight II* safeguards your valuable monitor from phosphor burn-in, an irreversible condition that occurs when the same image has been left onscreen for so long that it becomes permanently etched into the monitor glass.

Twilight II presents an elegant solution to this problem, automatically protecting your screen, by changing the image being displayed in many different selectable ways after you do not interact with the computer for a specified amount of time. You can select from variety of dazzling, full-color animation and special screen effect modules.

Twilight II is a Control Panel (CDev) for the Apple IIGS computer. *It* works with all GS/OS System 6.0 desktop programs such as the Finder, *AppleWorks GS*, *GraphicWriter III*, *Platinum Paint*, and many others: program switchers such as *The Manager* and *Switch-It!*, all text screen-based programs such as ProDOS 8 gems like *AppleWorks*

1

Classic and *ProTerm*, GS/OS text-based programs like *America Online*, and programs such as *Publish-It*.

Our goal is to make the best featured screen saver possible, enabling you to use your computer more productively. *Twilight II* 1.0 released in 1993 was in the making for over two years and represents an enormous amount of effort by many different people. This new version 2, first released in 2020, represents the efforts of many additional people.

In making this quality product available at a reasonable price without copy-protection, we hope that you will be supportive of our efforts by giving copies of *Twilight II* to your friends and family. Encourage them to purchase this updated manual from the publisher at: www.callapple.org/books. By supporting us, we will best be able to continue to support you and your computer into the future.

Features

Prevent Phosphor Burn In:

A permanent and real condition that happens when the same image is left on your monitor for too long!

Protection:

Twilight II supports and protects all your favorite desktop programs (*AppleWorks GS*, etc.), text mode-based programs (such as the GS/OS version of America Online, and ProDOS 8 programs like *AppleWorks* and *ProTerm*), and even other programs such as *Publish-It!*

Minimal Overhead:

Twilight II won't slow down you or the way your computer operates. Important operations such as file copying, printing, and file transfers will not be interrupted!

Ease of Use:

Our interface is the result of extensive testing and user feedback. Using the "Random Mode" feature, you can even select a different module to be run each time the screen is blanked!

Compatibility:

GS/OS System 6 is fully supported and required. *Twilight II* is compatible with all hardware and virtually all software for the Apple IIGS that follow Apple's guidelines! It works great with *The Manager* and *Switch-It*, as well as with RamFAST SCSI cards.

Phantom:

Via the included Phantom module, you can run all Phantasm modules from A.P.P.L.E./Quality Computers' Signature GS for compatibility.

Power:

Nothing else for the Apple IIGS can match *Twilight II's* screen-saving capabilities, over two years in the making and written in 100% assembly language for optimal speed and performance. Our effect module format is more flexible than the competition's, and even contains support for some features not found in other screen savers for any computer! A more powerful and versatile module format means better effects!

AppleShare Aware:

AppleTalk networks are fully supported!

Easy Installation:

Just point and click, using Apple's Installer program.

Effects

Nothing else can match the variety of effects included with *Twilight II*! What good is a screen saver that comes with only a few meager effects? We include over 65 different colorful and stunning screen saver effect modules:

Background Fader	LED Sign	Sega
Ball	Life	Sharks and Fish
Barney	Life, Meltdown	Short Out
Call-A.P.P.L.E.	Linealities	Snow
Clocks	MineHunt	Snowflakes
Color by Color	MiniFireworks	Spirals
Cyclone	Modern Art	Spirographics
Dissolve	Moiré	Static
Drip Drop	Mountains	String Art
Earth	Movie Theater	Strobe
Fading Clock	MultiTris	Swirls
Fazer	Perspective	Tiler
Fireworks	Phantom	Toast
Fireworks Silent	Plasma	Tunnel Game
Fish	PowerGrid	TunnelVision II
Flames	Puzzling	Twilight
Foreground Fader	Quotes	Universe
Globe	Reflections	Voting
Headlines	Rings	Wiper Blanker
Impulse 3-D	Ripple	Worms
Inverter	Roller	YouDrawIt!
Kaleidoscope	Scanner	
L.E.D. Message	Scroll	

REACHING US . . .

Please contact us if you have any questions, comments, or suggestions for improving *Twilight II*, or would like information on other A.P.P.L.E. programs, books and publications. We welcome your feedback and ideas.

Support of *Twilight II* and future versions, along with other products from Apple Pugetsound Program Library Exchange (A.P.P.L.E.), is available via:

Web: www.callapple.org

Books: www.callapple.org/books

Email: sales@callapple.org

Twitter: twitter.com/callapple

Facebook: www.facebook.com/APPLEug

TWILIGHT II'S DEVELOPMENT

Twilight II was originally written by the group Digital Youth Alliance. DYA was founded in January 1990 to join the efforts of several young people to create quality programs for the Apple IIGS.

DigiSoft Innovations is a small business formed in January 1992 by DYA, to handle marketing, distribution, and promotion of new DYA products, the first of which was *Twilight II*. Our original goal with DYA and Digisoft Innovations was to make it easier for our group of diehard Apple II hacker-enthusiasts who loved expanding the known 'limits' of the Apple IIGS, to excel in producing and distributing software in the fields of animation, sound, education, entertainment, and productivity

A.P.P.L.E. took over the *Twilight II* project in 2002 with the blessings of Jim Maricondo when he joined the A.P.P.L.E. restoration project. All images, documentation, source and binaries were provided to A.P.P.L.E. by DigiSoft Innovations at that time with the intention of creating a new version of *Twilight II*.

In April 2020, Antoine Vignau took over the main programming of the application in an effort, in combination with A.P.P.L.E.'s Bill Martens, Jim Maricondo and Brian Wiser, to produce a new version of *Twilight II* based on the original efforts. The result is this package which you are using now and its accompanying cover, logo and manual designed by Brian Wiser.

Source code for *Twilight II* is available from our A.P.P.L.E. Github page: https://github.com/callapple, and the program disk image is available at: https://www.callapple.org.

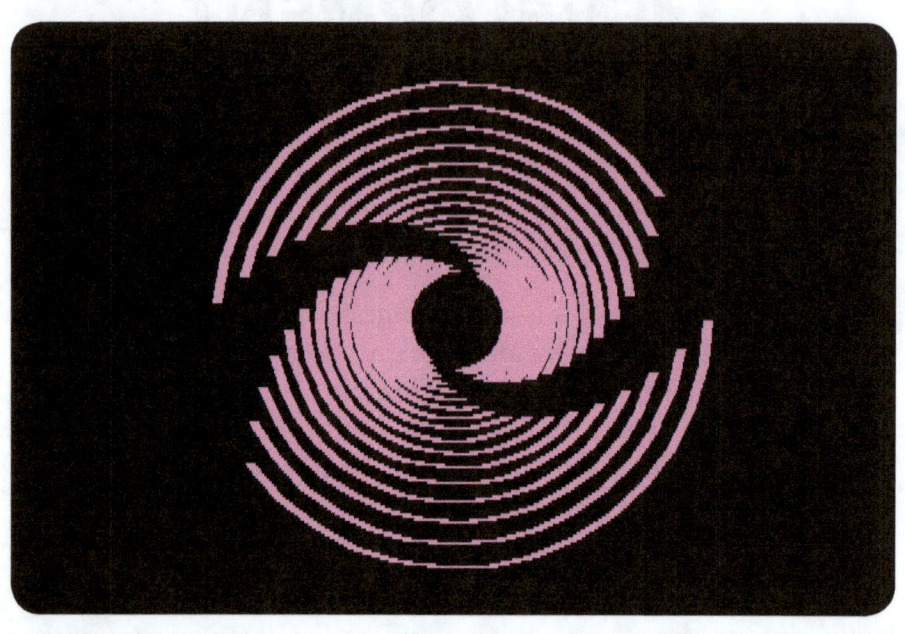

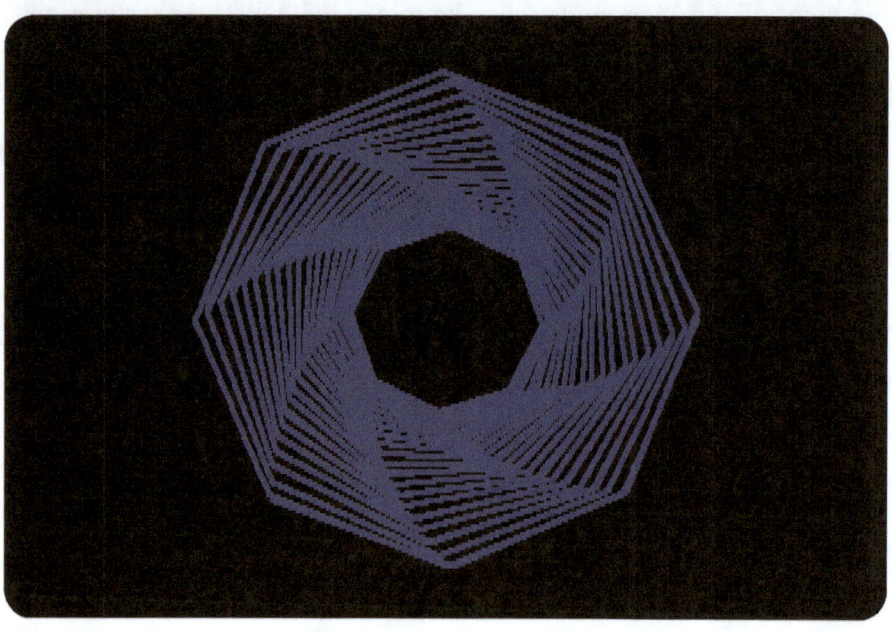

THANKS TO . . .

James C. Smith	Many awesome modules, installer scripts, Mac Classic, much more.
Derek Young	Support, writing some cool modules, KansasFest, great help at the October Expo!, etc.
Nathan Mates	Many cool modules, games and manual additions!
Joe Wankerl	KansasFest 1992 debugging sessions, feedback, testing.
Jim Murphy	DataField, help, phone calls, testing.
Matt Deatherage & Dave Lyons	Answering many questions and/or putting T2 through its paces!
Marc & Tammy Wolfgram & Collings	More ideas, support, booth sharing at AEE & AEW, great printing and fonts help.
Michael Lutynski	Testing, support, awesome T2 $C2 made with Animasia 3-D!
Dan Wellman	Support, feedback, DFest 1992, etc.
Steve 'Diz' Disbrow	GS+ support.
Matt Keller	Some great art, icons, support, etc.
Eric Shepherd	"Quotes" module, ideas.
Greg Templeman	Lots of bug feedback, ideas, "product champion!"
John Pothier	Most conscientious testing.

Seth Ober	
Mark Ranes	
Andy Polk	
Chuck Newby	Beta testing.
Bryan "Zak"	HIG advice too.
Joe Schober	AO support too.
Jim Mensch	Core of "Tiler."
Dan Zimmerman	System 6 support, testing.
Andy Wells	More ideas, testing.
Dino Bagdadi	Ideas, testing.
Scott Gentry & Marty Knight	AOL Apple II Forums support.
Joe Kohn	Shareware Solutions support.
Ewen Wannop	Updated Spectrum *Twilight II* XCMD.
John K. Morris	Source code recovery assistance.
Bill Martens & Brian Wiser	Planning and executing the 2020 release of *Twilight II* v2.0.

And thanks to **You**,
our **Customers**,
our fantastic **Beta Testers**,

and anyone accidentally forgotten who helped in this massive undertaking!

CREDITS . . .

Twilight II Control Panel – Jim R. Maricondo

Version 2.0 Build and Release – Antoine Vignau

IPC Technical Documentation – Antoine Vignau

Help Screens – Bill Martens, Antoine Vignau

Twilight II v2.0 Manual – Brian Wiser, Bill Martens, Jim R. Maricondo, Antoine Vignau

Twilight II Logo, Cover, Manual Design and Layout – Brian Wiser

---

Installer Scripts – James C. Smith, Antoine Vignau

Color by Color, Cyclone, Drip Drop, Fading Clock, Fireworks, Headlines, Inverter, Life, Mountains, Plasma, Reflections, Roller, Scanner, Scroll, Short Out, Snow, S.L.E.D., String Art, TunnelVision II, Twilight – James C. Smith

Earth, Impulse 3-D, Meltdown, Moiré, Spirographics, Strobe, Universe, YouDrawIt! – Jim R. Maricondo

Sound Patcher – Jim R. Maricondo

Movie Theater, Phantom – Jim R. Maricondo, Derek Young

Dissolve, Kaleidoscope, Static – Derek Young

Puzzling, Worms – Jim R. Maricondo, Jonah Stich

Tiler – Jim R. Maricondo, Jim Mensch

Quotes – Eric Shepherd

Clocks, Fish, Flames Globe, L.E.D Message, Linealities, MiniFireworks, Modern Art, MultiTris, Perspective, Power Grid, Sharks and Fish, Snowflakes, Spirals, Swirls, Toast, Tunnel Game, Voting – Nathan Mates

DataField Control DefProc – Jim Murphy III

Pascal Sample Module (Shapes) – Josef Wankerl

Rings – Chris McKinsey, Jim R. Maricondo

Ripple – Michael Searl, Neon Software

STARTING OUT

Introduction

Before attempting to use *Twilight II*, please at least glance through this section first so that *Twilight II* is installed properly and you have a general idea of what is happening. This will save you much time in the long run.

Twilight II employs the concept of screen saver modules. When it is time to blank the screen so that burn-in does not occur, in a GS/OS desktop-based program, *Twilight II* will use the currently selected module (or a randomly selected module if random mode is activated.) Each module is responsible for the effect performed when the screen is blanked (e.g. Fireworks, Mountains, Snow, etc.)

It is your choice which modules you want to install – if you want to install them all, or install some or none of them. If you choose to install no modules, however, the screen will always be made pitch black when it is time to blank and no special effects or animations will be possible. The only advantage to not installing all the modules is that *Twilight II* will take up less space on disk.

Twilight II also is able to run all *Phantasm* effects through a *Twilight II* module called Phantom. If you are a *Signature GS* owner upgrading to *Twilight II*, you can still use all your old effects!

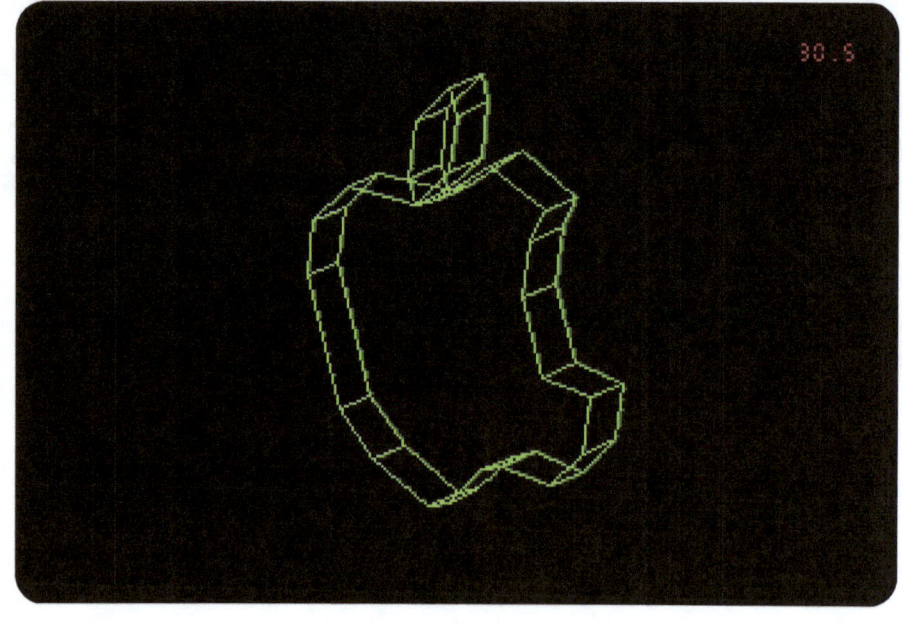

VITAL INFORMATION

Terminology and Conventions

Keys on the keyboard are referenced in italics by the name printed on them (e.g. *Shift*, *Option*, *J*, etc.) The *Open-Apple* key is referred to as the *Command* key.

Names of disks, files and directories (folders) on disk are printed in italics.

Keyboard equivalents, where available, for controls and buttons on screen are listed to the right of the titles of the controls. Steps to follow are indented and numbered. For example:

1. Purchase *Twilight II*.
2. Use the Installer for easy installation onto your system.
3. Never worry about screen burn-in!

Requirements

To use *Twilight II* you need:

- An Apple IIGS.

- GS/OS System 6.01 or later.

- CFFA3000 or other mass storage device with multi-partition capability and at least 32MB free space.

- A minimum of 100k RAM free for use by *Twilight II*. (A good indication of how much free memory you have available can be obtained by selecting "About the Finder..." and noting the display of available memory.)

While 1.125 megabytes of memory might suffice on a stripped down system, to best use *Twilight II*, 1.5 megabytes of memory or more is recommended. The more Desk Accessories, INITs, Control Panels, and system sounds you use, the less free memory will be available for use by *Twilight II*.

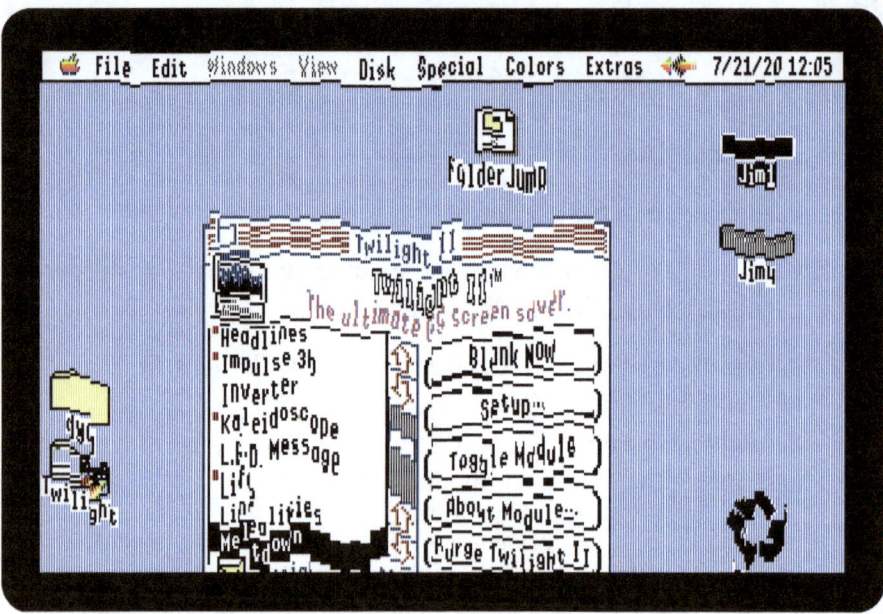

INSTALLING
TWILIGHT II

Module Concept Overview

For a module to show up in the available module list when the *Twilight II* control panel is opened, it must be present in the *Twilight* folder, which must be located in the same directory as the *Twilight.II* control panel. The Installer scripts take care of all this for you, while allowing you to customize the installation to your particular setup and tastes. After initial installation, should you decide you wish to delete a module, all you have to do is use a utility program such as the Finder to delete the appropriate module in the *Twilight* folder.

Before You Go On . . .

If you are a developer who wants to create your own modules for *Twilight II*, we recommend you read the Technical Reference section beginning on page 65.

Installation Options

There are several different ways in which you can install *Twilight II*. Each installation option is controlled by an Installer script. Which script to choose depends mainly on your hardware setup. Apple IIGS System 6 must be installed beforehand. If you do not install *Twilight II* on your startup (boot) disk, then *Twilight II* will not automatically be installed every time you start your computer.

Twilight II comes on one 32MB digital disk image from www.callapple.org, which can be copied to a CFFA3000 or other mass storage partition with CiderPress.

Twilight II (startup disk)

If you have a hard drive with System 6 installed and enough free disk space (about 2 megabytes), we recommend this script be used. The selected disk must be a startup disk. Technically, this script does the following: ('*' represents the volume name of the boot disk that you have selected)

- *Twilight.II* screen saver control panel is copied to the **:System:CDevs* folder

- All the *Twilight II* effect modules are copied to a new **:System:CDevs:Twilight* folder; where separate sound and no-sound versions of a module exist, the module with sound is copied

- *Twilight II* Finder icons are copied to the **:Icons* folder

- *Twilight II* Clock Font, used by default in the Clock module, is copied to the **:System:Fonts* folder

- *Twilight II* YouDrawIt! module's included animation template files (ATF's) are copied to the **:System:CDevs:Twilight:YDI. Animations* folder

- All included freeware effects for use with the Phantom module are copied to the **:System:CDevs:Twilight:Phantom. Effects* folder

Twilight II (any location)

This script is very similar to the above one, except that most files are copied to a folder you specify. You should use this script if you don't have enough room on your boot disk, or if you do not want *Twilight II* to be automatically installed every time you boot your computer. This script technically does the following:

- *Twilight.II* screen saver control panel is copied to the folder you have selected

- All *Twilight II* effect modules are copied to the *Twilight* folder which is created in the directory you selected, where separate sound and no-sound versions of a module exist, the module with sound is copied

- *Twilight II* Finder icons are copied to the *Icons* folder of the disk used to boot your computer

- *Twilight II* Clock Font is copied to the *System:Fonts* folder of the boot disk.

- *Twilight II* YouDrawIt! module's included animation template files (ATF's) are copied to a new *Twilight:YDI.Animations* folder, in the directory you specified

- All included freeware effects for use with the Phantom module are copied to the **:System:CDevs:Twilight:Phantom.Effects* folder

- *Twilight II* Life modules included pattern files (ATF's) are copied to the **:System:CDevs:Twilight:Life.Patterns* folder

Twilight II (no modules)

This script installs the minimum amount of files needed to use *Twilight II*. We recommend you use this script if your boot disk has very little space, but you still want *Twilight II* to be copied to it (so it can be automatically installed every time you boot.) The selected disk must be a startup disk. This script should be used in conjunction with one or more of the scripts for individual modules. Technically, this script does the following:

- *Twilight.II* screen saver control panel is copied to the **:System:CDevs* folder

- *Twilight II* Finder icons are copied to the **:Icons* folder

- All included freeware effects for use with the Phantom module are copied to the **:System:CDevs:Twilight:Phantom.Effects* folder

Sound Control Panel Patcher

This script installs a copy of our Sound Patcher program in the directory you select. This program allows you to painlessly modify your copy of Apple's System 6 Sound control panel so that you can assign sounds to play for "Screen Blanking" and "Screen Un-blanking" events. See "Using Sound Patcher" for more instructions.

The only way to install Sound Patcher from the Installer is by using this script. No other scripts install the Sound Patcher program.

Signature Phantasm Effects

Via *Twilight II*'s versatile Phantom module, all Phantasm effects can be used with *Twilight II*! Only people who also own *Signature GS* should use this script, as it requires your original *Signature GS* disk. This script accomplishes the following:

- 7 Phantasm effects are copied from the *:Signature:Effects* folder to a new **:System:CDevs:Twilight:Phantom.Effects* directory. These effects can now be selected for use with the *Twilight II* Phantom module.

Scripts for Individual Modules

Each of these scripts installs one screen saver effect module onto the startup disk you select. (The module is copied to the **:System:CDevs:Twilight* folder.) Some modules have sound and no-sound versions (e.g. Fireworks), because digitized sound files take up extra space, the no-sound versions are also provided for people trying to conserve disk space.

Scripts for Individual Animation Template Files

Each of these scripts installs one animation template file (ATF) onto the startup disk you select. ATF's are animation images used by the YouDrawIt! (YDI) module. (The selected ATF is copied to the *System:CDevs:Twilight:YDI.Animations* folder of the volume you select.) The scripts for Blank.ATF and Blank.EATF install blank templates that you can use to create your own animation. See the YouDrawIt! section of this manual for more information.

Using the Installer

To use the Installer to easily install *Twilight II*, do the following:

1. Download the 32MB digital disk image from www.callapple.org.

2. Copy the disk image to your CFFA3000 or other mass storage device using CiderPress.

3. Start up your Apple IIGS as you normally do.

4. Go to the *Twilight II* mass storage partition.

5. Open the "Twilight" folder and launch the Installer program. The main window will soon appear, as pictured below.

6. Select the script or scripts you want installed from the list of available scripts.

7. Use the disk button to select the disk you wish to have *Twilight II* or its modules installed upon. Some scripts will require you to select a folder to copy the files to. Feel free to click help on any script for additional help information.

8. Click the install button to install the selected script or scripts.

9. After *Twilight II* has been installed successfully, click the quit button, restart the computer, and remove the original *Twilight II* disk image, putting it in a safe place.

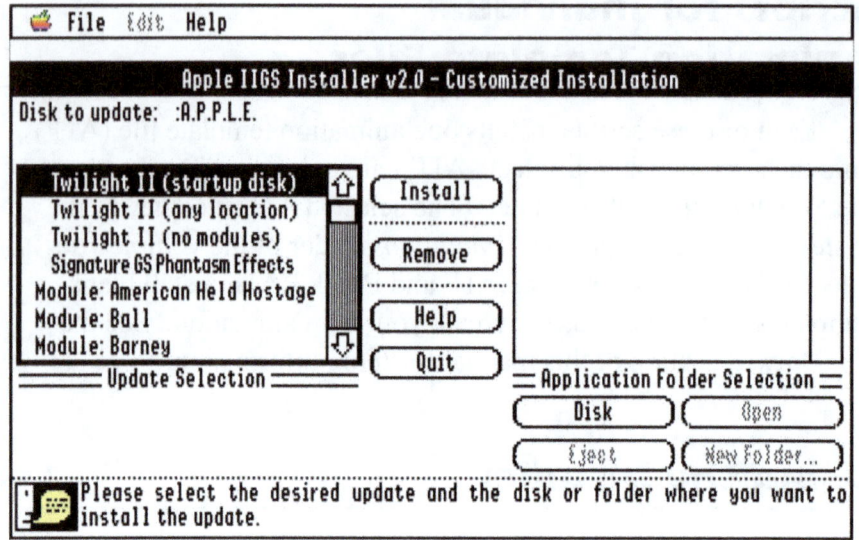

Using Sound Patcher

Sound Patcher is a simple program that allows you to harmlessly modify the Sound control panel that comes with System 6 to allow the assigning of specific sounds to "Screen Blanking" and "Screen Un-blanking" events. *Twilight II* generates these events whenever the desktop or text screens blank or un-blank, with only two exceptions. First, when you preview a module by clicking "Blank Now" from the main window, these sounds will not be generated. Also, the sounds will not be played when you are running a ProDOS 8 program and the text screen blanks. Using *Sound Patcher* is easy:

1. Start up your Apple IIGS as you normally do.
2. Launch the *Sound.Patcher* program, wherever you instructed the Installer to put it, or from directly off the *Twilight II* partition on your mass storage device. "Patch..." from the File menu will automatically be chosen.
3. Locate the *Sound* control panel in the *CDevs* folder of your boot disk, select it, and click open.

In a few short moments, the operation will be complete. You now can open the Sound control panel and assign sounds to your two new *Twilight II* events.

Spectrum XCMD and *Twilight II* Control

Included in the base distribution is a *Spectrum* XCMD by Ewen Wannop which is an update to the *Twilight II* XCMD which shipped with *Spectrum 2.1*, an FTP program. You do not need *Spectrum* to run *Twilight II*, this is just an update to provide better control over it. If a version of *Spectrum* later than 2.1 is already on your system, this XCMD should be on there, and you do not need to install it.

If not, you can download the latest version of *Spectrum*. Read the documentation contained in the "SpectrumXCMD" folder in this distribution, and copy the XCMD from that hierarchy to the XCMDs folder under the "Addons" directory where you installed *Spectrum* to.

For more information about XCMD, read the *Spectrum* manual as well as the "IPC Module Commands" on page 95.

ACTIVATING TWILIGHT II

If Twilight II (startup disk) or
Twilight II (no modules) Script was Used

After installation, *Twilight II* will be located in the *System:CDevs* folder of your boot disk. *Twilight II* will be automatically activated during boot and ready to use after you restart your computer.

For future reference, you can prevent *Twilight II* from loading by holding down the Control key when you start the computer. This will be visually indicated by a red X being drawn over the *Twilight II* boot-up icon.

If Twilight II (my location) Script Was Used

Twilight II will be located in the folder you have chosen. You will have to manually activate *Twilight II* each time you boot your computer. You can do this by double-clicking from the Finder the *Twilight.II* control panel icon wherever you chose to have it installed. This will also open the main *Twilight II* window at the same time .

After *Twilight II* has been activated, you must keep the disk it is on write-enabled for *Twilight II* to function correctly.

OPENING
THE MAIN WINDOW

At any time after *Twilight II* has been activated, to open the main *Twilight II* window, follow these steps:

1. Choose the Control Panels item from the Apple menu.
2. Click the *Twilight II* icon to select it.
3. Click the Open button.

Alternatively, if the "Install T2 NDA" option is on, you can simply select the *Twilight II* item from the Apple menu.

As a shortcut, you can also press *Command-Control-T*, *Command-~* or *Command-'* to open up the main window. (These equivalents are only available when not already in use by the application running when you press them.) The System 6 Control Panels desk accessory must always be installed for *Twilight II* to operate, with no exception.

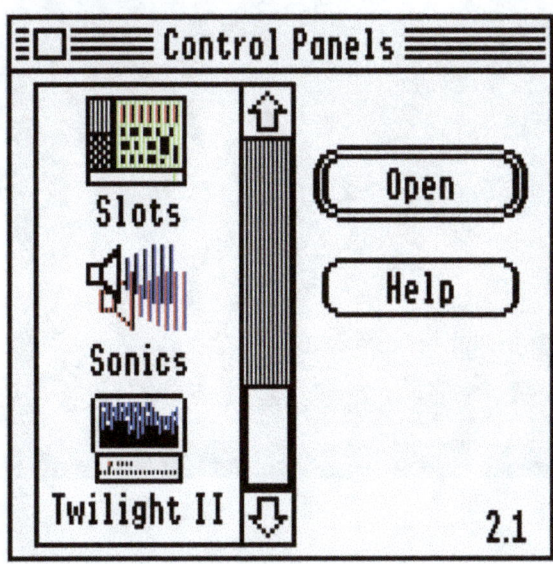

REFERENCE

This section describes every aspect of *Twilight II* in detail. If you have any questions about a particular feature, the answers are probably here. Once you have familiarized yourself with a few concepts, using *Twilight II* will become largely intuitive. Refer to this section when any questions arise.

There are a few frequently used terms and ideas that will benefit you by familiarizing yourself with. You might want to quickly glance over a few concepts presented in this section before fully experimenting with *Twilight II*.

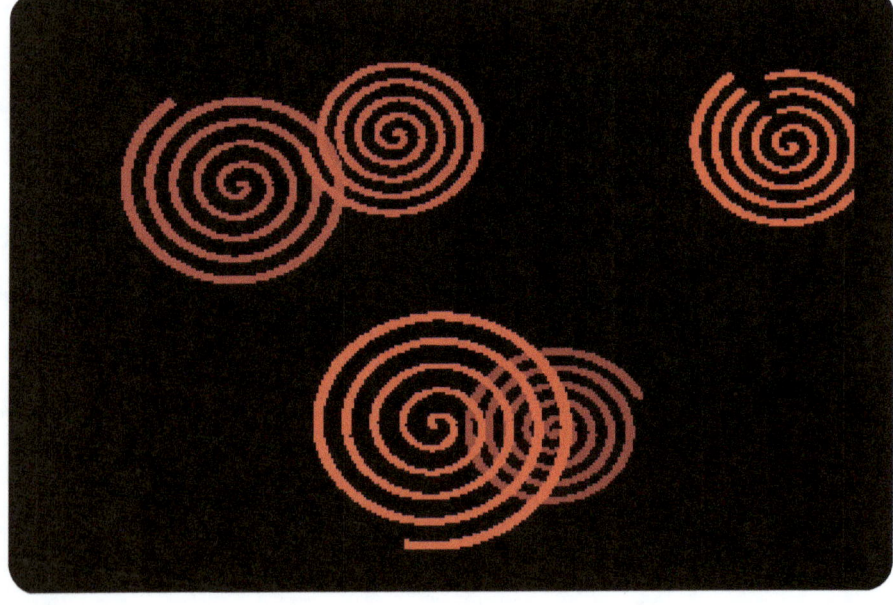

KEY CONCEPTS & TERMS

When your Apple IIGS has not been used (interacted with) for the amount of time specified in Setup: Options, *Twilight II* blanks (animates or moves around) the screen to protect your costly monitor from permanent phosphor bum-in, a condition that occurs when the same image has been left on screen for too long a time.

Types of Screen Blanks

There are two distinct types of screen blanks:

Background Blank

The screen is made entirely black (i.e. no special effects or animations are run) and the program you were using continues running. So, if you were printing or copying files when the screen blanked, the printing or copying will not be interrupted. Background blanking is used all the time in text mode-based programs.

Foreground Blank

The screen is blanked using the effect module you have most recently chosen and the program you were in stops running. Because foreground blanking takes control of the computer, if you were printing or copying files when *Twilight II* kicked in, the printing or copying would be interrupted and would not continue until the screen was un-blanked (i.e. a key was hit, the mouse moved, etc.) Foreground blanking is not available in programs that use the text screen; foreground blanking is only used in desktop-based programs that run under GS/OS.

You can have the best of both worlds in regard to background versus foreground blanking. See "Options: Watch Cursor" in the next section.

Compatibility

Twilight II is very AppleTalk and AppleShare friendly. It can be run off a network without interference with network communication. Also, when a server shuts down, *Twilight II* will not crash or hang.

Being very stable, *Twilight II* should not interfere with any applications. The screen can be blanked under the few different types of programs below.

Mouse screen corners can be used in all of the types of programs below. However, corners assigned to foreground blank now will only work in desktop-based programs. Also, when corners are used in other than desktop-based programs, you must position the mouse *exactly* in the corner to achieve the desired result. We are investigating workarounds to make this easier for the future.

Desktop-Based

Desktop-based programs run under GS/OS and are easily identified by the standard Apple menu bar, interface look and feel. Examples include: *GraphicWriter III*, *Platinum Paint*, *AppleWorks GS*, *Finder*, *Installer*, *ShrinkIt-GS*, *Universe Master*, *Foundation*, *Switch-It*, and many others. *Twilight II* is most flexible under such programs – both background and foreground blanks are possible.

Text Mode-Based

Text mode-based programs can run under either GS/OS or ProDOS 8. The classic desk accessory menu that appears when you press *Command-Control-Escape* is an example of text mode, as are *America Online*, *AppleWorks* Classic, *ProTerm*, the *Orca/M* shell, and many more. In text mode-based programs, *Twilight II* will automatically perform a background blank when the computer has not been interacted with for the amount of time specified. Foreground blanking is not possible, so you will never notice any special effects being performed by *Twilight II* in text mode-based programs.

Low-Res, High-Res, and Double High-Res Mode-Based

ProDOS 8 programs, such as *Publish-It!*, that use the low-resolution, high-resolution, or double high-resolution graphics modes can also be blanked by *Twilight II*. When it is time to blank, *Twilight II* will clear the screen to black in the background, thus allowing the program running to routine. No special effects will be performed in these programs in order to ensure full compatibility.

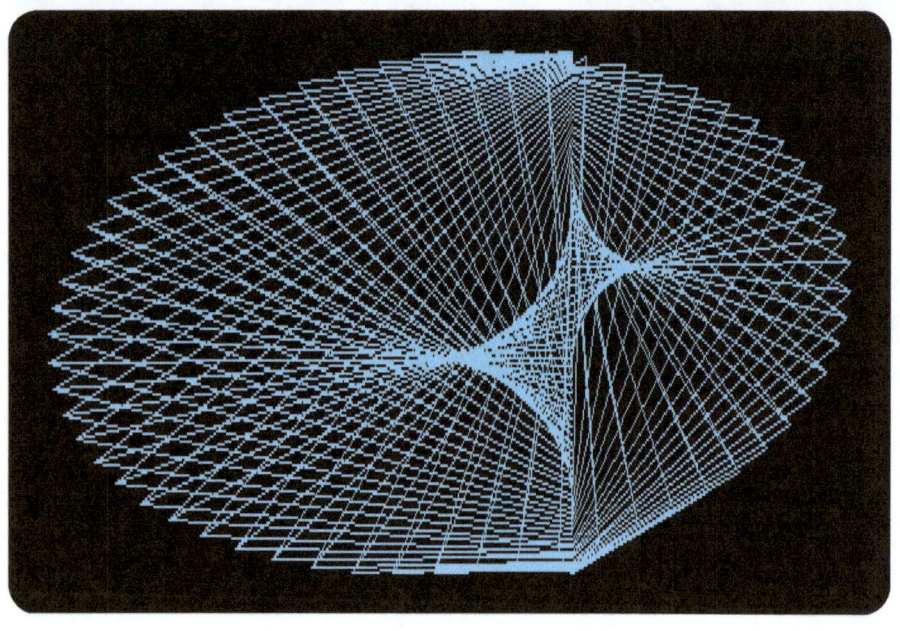

USING TWILIGHT II

Each time *Twilight II* is opened you will see a window similar to the picture at the bottom of this page.

The Main Window

Changes made to *Twilight II*'s main window will not take effect until the window is closed. For instance, if you turn on random mode or make *Twilight II* temporarily inactive, these changes will not take effect until the main window is closed.

Unfortunately, at times this logic can be somewhat confusing until you adjust to it. For instance, if you previously had the Fireworks module selected and then you open up *Twilight II*, select Cyclone, and move to a foreground blank now corner, the screen will blank using Fireworks, not Cyclone, because the module change does not take effect until the main window is closed.

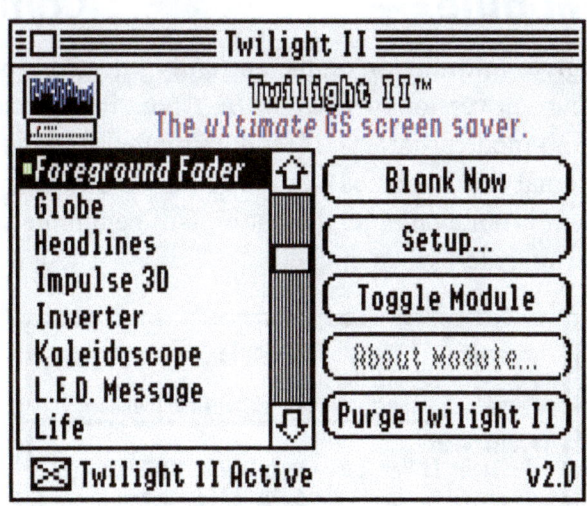

List of Installed Modules

The names of all the modules currently installed in the *Twilight* folder will appear in this list. The currently selected module, or modules if random mode is on, will be highlighted. Two modules will always be present in this list (even when the *Twilight* module folder is empty) because they are internally built in – their names are italicized to denote this. These modules are Background Fader and Foreground Fader.

Background Fader is special because it always does a background blank (allowing the program running to continue after the screen has been set to black by *Twilight II*) when the time to blank has elapsed, instead of blanking in the foreground (where the program running would be interrupted until the screen is un-blanked.) For this reason, Background Fader is also underlined.

Foreground Fader will also make the screen black, but like all modules (other than Background Fader) it will interrupt the program running when *Twilight II* blanks the screen in a desktop-based program. **NOTE**: Any modules in the list that appear dimmed (gray and not selectable) all the time are not compatible with your version of *Twilight II*.

About Module   Command-?

This control gives information on the currently selected module and displays the current version of *Twilight II*. About information is not available in 320-mode programs, if random mode is on, the selected module is internal (i.e. italicized), or the setup window is open. When about module it is not available, the button will be dimmed or will produce a warning alert when clicked.

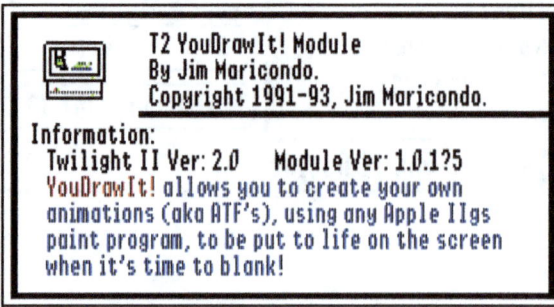

34

Blank Now   Command-B

Blank now gives you a preview of the currently selected module's special effects. Previews are not available when random mode is on, so blank now will appear dimmed (un-selectable) at such times.

Setup   Command-S

Clicking on the setup control will open the *Twilight II* setup window which allows you to configure how each module operates to suit your tastes . Not all modules support being set up, but most do. You can set up each module independently of every other – so when you change the setup of one module, the setups of the other modules aren't lost. In addition, if you boot your Apple IIGS off of a multi-user AppleShare network, each user can have their own, independent set of *Twilight II* preferences that don't interfere with anyone else's!

Setup data under normal conditions is saved in a file called *Twilight. Setup* in the *Twilight* module folder. (If you are on an AppleShare network, it is saved to your user folder on the server.)

Setup is only available in 640-mode desktop programs. When not available, the setup control will appear dimmed or will produce a warning alert. If setup is clicked when random mode is off and a module that supports setup is selected, then *Twilight II* will directly open the setup screen for that module. Otherwise the setup window will be opened up to the corners screen.

Purge Twilight II   Command-P

This control allows you to quickly remove *Twilight II* from memory. After pressing purge *Twilight II*, your computer will behave like *Twilight II* was not installed (as if you held down Control during boot to prevent *Twilight II* from loading, or if *Twilight II* was not installed in your boot disk's *CDevs* folder at all).

This option only affects memory- *Twilight II* is not deleted from your disk! To reactivate *Twilight II*, you can either reboot, select the *Twilight II* icon from the Control Panels desk accessory, or double-click on the *Twilight II* icon in the Finder.

Random Mode   Command-R

Random mode is only available if you booted (started) the computer off of a hard disk drive or ROMDisk. When random mode is turned on, you can then select several different modules from the available module list, and each time *Twilight II* blanks the screen (in a desktop program) a different module's effect will be used! The Background Fader module, due to its nature, is not available when random mode is on and as such will appear dimmed. To select more than one module, click the mouse while holding down the *Command* key. To select a range of modules, experiment clicking with *Shift* pressed.

Some modules may behave differently or have special options when run from random mode. Short out, for instance, will short the screen to black and then immediately run the next random module when random mode is active. Otherwise it will short the screen to black and delay until a key has been pressed. For more information, refer to "Random Mode Special Behavior" under "Other Information" on page 54.

Twilight II Active   Command-T

This control allows you to temporarily turn off *Twilight II*. The screen will not blank once *Twilight II* is inactivated in this fashion, but all memory allocated by *Twilight II* will be kept in use.

Toggling this option is the functional equivalent of pressing *Shift-Clear* until the border color flashes. See "Miscellaneous Features: Temporary Deactivation" for more information on this feature.

ⓘ **Note**: The status of this option is not saved to disk. The next time you turn on or restart your computer, *Twilight II* will automatically default to being active again.

The Setup Window

The setup window, shown below with the options screen, provides a great deal of flexibility in customizing *Twilight II*. Two setup screens are built into *Twilight II* and will always be available: Options and Screen Corners. Other setup screens will depend on which modules you have installed. Three controls will always be available at the top of the setup window:

Setup

The setup popup control is used to select the module to be configured. After a module is selected from the Setup control, you can make changes to the controls created that will affect the operation of the module.

Save   Command-S

After you have made changes to a module's setup screen, you must click the save button for your changes to be remembered. This takes a little while getting used to, but it allows you the flexibility of not saving your changes if you ever mess up.

Twilight II can remind you when your new settings have not been saved (see "Warning Alerts" later in this chapter). Save will not be enabled (selectable) until you have modified a setup screen.

Test   Command-T

The test button allows you to instantly see your setup changes will affect a module. Upon clicking test, first your changes are saved, and then a blank now of the module being set up is performed. Test will not be enabled when configuring screen corners or options.

Screen Corners

The screen corners setup screen, depicted below, allows you to give each of the four corners of the screen a specific function. There is a slight delay of a couple seconds before *Twilight II* will react to the mouse being placed in a corner. Four functions can be assigned:

Disabled

Twilight II doesn't behave any differently when the mouse is in the corner.

Never Blank

Twilight II will never blank the screen when the mouse is in the corner. The cursor will change into a little crossed out *Twilight II* icon to visually indicate this.

(Foreground) Blank Now

Twilight II will blank the screen immediately using the currently active effect module (the module that was last selected when the main window was closed, or a random module if random mode is on.) The program that was running will be halted and will not resume until it is time to un-blank the screen.

Background Blank Now

Twilight II will immediately fade the screen to black, but the program that was running is not stopped. So, if you go to a background blank now corner while copying files in the Finder, the screen will fade to black but the copy will not stop. With foreground blank now, the copy would have stopped until the screen is restored.

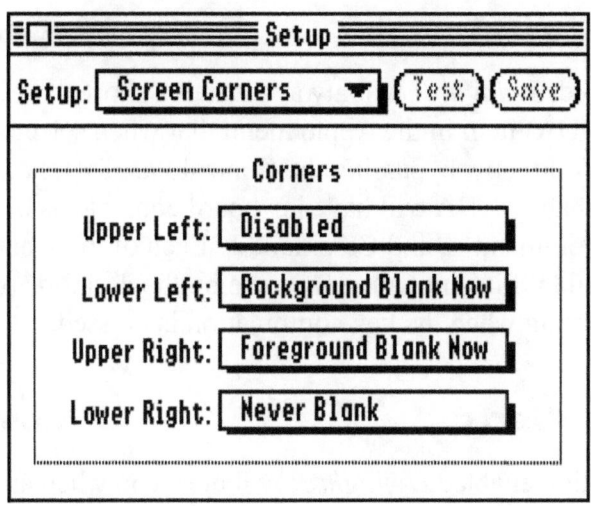

Options

This setup screen allows you to customize many features and aspects of *Twilight II*. There features are as follows, with keyboard equivalents where available listed to the right of the feature name:

Mouse Movement   Command-D
Un-blanks Desktop

When this control is unchecked, the mouse will not be allowed to restore the screen after the screen has blanked in desktop-based programs.

Menu Bar Box   Command-M

When checked, *Twilight II* will flash a small black square in the upper right corner of the top menu bar of desktop-based programs to alert you that it is active. This square might seem to visually appear to interfere with some programs that have many menus spanning across the entire screen but no permanent damage can ever be caused.

Install T2 NDA   Command-I

When checked, *Twilight II* will always install a shortcut new desk accessory (NDA) item in the Apple menu that when selected will open up *Twilight II* directly, bypassing the Control Panel's desk accessory. *Twilight II's* handy NDA will have keyboard equivalents of Command-Control-T, Command-~, and Command-'. Each of these equivalents is only available if it is not already in use by the desktop application currently running when the key combination is pressed.

Warning Alerts   Command-A

With this option enabled, *Twilight II* will alert you when any of the following situations occur:

- A setup screen has been modified and the changes have not been saved.

- Blank now has been pressed but the caps lock key is down and the caps lock "lock" option is on.

- Purge Twilight II has been pressed.

- Setup or about module has been clicked in a 320-mode desktop program.

- Setup has been clicked and the currently selected module does not support setup.

Prohibit Sound   Command-P

Many modules have sound effects to accompany their effects. While these sounds normally can be toggled on and off in each specific module's setup screen, this option enables you to quickly and easily prohibit sound use in all modules at once.

Low Memory Mode   Command-L

Low memory mode was designed for users with low memory. With low memory mode on, *Twilight II* uses 32k less memory than normal. The only disadvantages are that some modules might run slightly slower, and the few modules, such as Impulse 3-D, that require a special feature called shadowing to work right will be slightly more likely to produce error messages when run.

Beeping Un-blanks   Command-B

Through this option, *Twilight II* can be told to un-blank when your computer beeps. If the screen has been background blanked, in either a desktop-based or text mode-based program, and the application running emits a system beep (which may cause a specific sound effect to be played if the System 6 Sound control panel is installed), *Twilight II* will un-blank the screen when this option is on. This option may not work with every program, but virtually all Apple IIGS-specific software should be compatible.

Use QuickResponse   Command-Q

Twilight II incorporates a revolutionary new method to detect key presses without interfering with your computer and the way you use it. However, this technique requires that you must be using a ROM01 or ROM03 Apple IIGS and an Apple Desktop Bus (ADB) keyboard, such as the detached keyboard that came with your computer. If these requirements are not met, you should not have this option enabled.

Caps Lock "Lock"   Command-C

When checked, the position of the *caps lock* key becomes important, because it 'locks' the current state of the screen when it is in the down position. With this option on, if the screen is un-blanked and the caps lock key is pressed down, the screen will never blank until *caps lock* is returned to the up position. Similarly, if the screen is blanked and the caps lock key is down, the screen will not un-blank until *caps lock* is released.

This is a very versatile feature. One nifty use is to use *caps lock* to stop the screen from accidentally un-blanking. For instance, you might want to watch the snow fill up your desktop. Use this feature to stop you from accidentally restoring the screen (and stopping the snow!)

Text Screen Blank

Use this option to tell *Twilight II* which types of text mode-based programs you want the screen to be background blanked in. The following options are available: blank all programs that use the text screen (e.g. *AppleWorks, ProTerm, America Online*, etc.), or only blank GS/OS text mode-based programs, or never blank text mode-based programs.

DoubleClick Function

What double-clicking on a module's name (in the list of modules on the main *Twilight II* window) will do can be adjusted with this control. Double-clicks can either be ignored, set to "blank now" using the module double-clicked upon, set to select the module and close *Twilight II*, or set to setup the selected module. If you have the latter selected and then double-click on a module that does not support setup, *Twilight II* will select the "Screen Corners" setup screen for you.

Watch Cursor

Twilight II can be set to behave differently when the on-screen cursor (in desktop programs) is a watch. *Twilight II* can either never blank in these cases, or automatically background blank, or be ignored so that a regular blank occurs (blank normally). This is a very powerful feature.

With this option set to background blank, you could be in the Finder and walk away while it's doing nothing, and a normal blank would occur (using the active effect module.) Then you could instruct the Finder to copy some files and walk away, and automatically since the cursor has turned to a watch, *Twilight II* will do a background blank so the copy can continue. (Similar situations happen during many other operations such as printing with most programs, or shrinking and unshrinking files with *ShrinkIt-GS*.)

As you can probably tell, in most instances you will want to leave this option set to background blank. But there are a few special instances when you may want to have *Twilight II* set to not blank when a watch cursor is on-screen. Some older Apple printer drivers will not like the screen being made black during printing and will print a constant stream of black after the screen has background blanked during printing. If you notice this happening you will want to set this option to never blank.

Minutes Before Blanking

This control allows you to set the default number of minutes of no activity that Twilight II will let elapse before automatically blanking the screen. To change the value, you may either press the up-arrow and down-arrow on the keyboard or click on the little up and down-arrow icons.

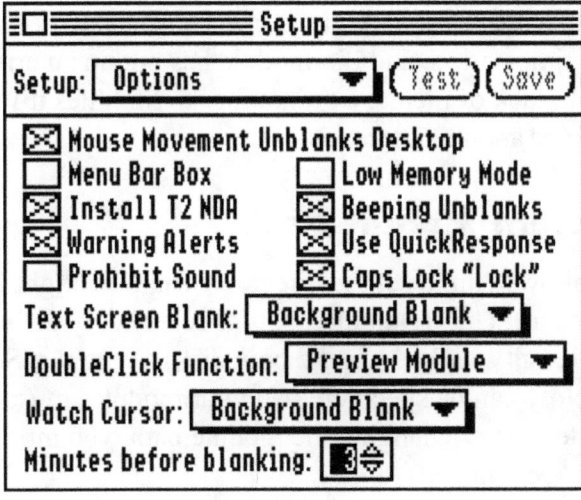

The "Setup" window with *Options* selected

Advanced Options

SHR Corners Active

When this option is enabled (checked), the screen corners as set up in the Setup:Screen Corners are honored. When unchecked, that is the equivalent of setting all four corners to disabled.

Swap Modules Every XX:YY minutes

This option lets you force a module change after a specified amount of time in a foreground blank. If there are multiple modules toggled active, and the current one has been active for the specified time, it will exit and another random module from those toggled will be run. Certain modules that do small things like Short Out may exit before the specified time period, and if a module has put up an error message (usually due to lack of memory or inability to find files it wants) will always exit after about 25 seconds.

Use Different Module Path

This option allows you to set the directory where Twilight II looks for all its modules in. The "(Default)" path is selected by default, and is *:System:CDevs:Twilight: (* is the boot disk). With the 'Set It' button, another directory can be specified. All your modules must reside in the same folder. After changing the module path, you must reboot for Twilight II to recognize it.

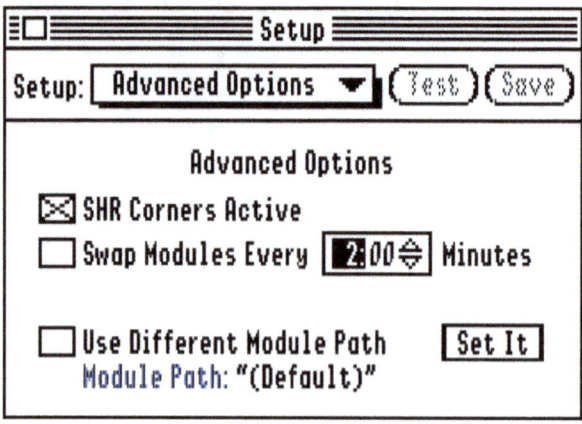

ENHANCED MODULES

The setup screens of each installed module will vary. Most options are self-explanatory for the most part, but a few modules require extra elaboration:

Cyclone

It is possible to add, modify, and delete preset animations for the Cyclone module if you are a programmer or adept with a resource editor. Cyclone uses one word to store all its setup information. Seven options are packed into that one word. They are defined as follows:

IsPreset	Bit 15	Indicates if the current setup options are the same as one of the preset options.
Width	Bits 14-12	Legal values are 0-7.
Shape	Bits 11-8	Legal values are 1-10.
VerticalMirror	Bit 7	Indicates if the Vertical Mirror is on.
Length	Bits 6-4	Legal values are 1-7. 1 = Infinite. 2 = Length of 15 lines, 3 = Length of 30 lines, etc.
HorizontalMirror	Bit 3	Indicates if the Horizontal Mirror is on.
Color	Bits 2-0	Legal values are 0-7.

The easiest way to determine what the value of this word would be for any given set of parameters is to simply configure Cyclone to the desired settings and then look at the saved configuration word in the *Twilight.Setup* file (stored in the *Twilight* module folder.)

To make an animation configuration into a new preset for Cyclone you must first add a new menu item to the preset menu, with an ID of the Cyclone configuration word just created above. The `IsPreset` bit (bit 15) should *never* be set in the menu item ID because Cyclone keeps track of this for itself. The following is an example using Genesys.

1. Bring up the Cyclone options from within *Twilight II*. Set the options to the values you want for your new preset. For this example we will set width to 8,length to infinite, color to sliding. shape to diamond and both mirrors to off. Click save to save the new setup information to disk.

2. Launch Genesys and open the Twilight.Setup file.

3. Select rType $1002 in the type list on the left and then double click on Cyclone config in the resource list on the right. The generic resource data window should open up and show the value $10 $7C. Adjusting for Apple IIGS reverse hex; the actual Value 'of the Cyclone setup word is $7C10. Remember this.

4. Close all the open windows and then open Cyclone, also located in your *Twilight* folder.

5. Select menu in the type list on the left and then double click on the preset menu in the resource list on the right. (You will have to figure out which menu resource is the preset menu by looking at each one until you find it.)

6. Select Add Item from the Options menu to add a new menu item to the Preset menu.

7. Make sure your new item is selected. Then select edit item data from the options menu. Type in the value of the configuration word into the item ID field, $7C10 for this example. Click on the change button to accept the new ID.

8. Double click on the new menu item and then type in a name for your new preset. We will use Diamond.

Close the preset menu window, pick "Save" from the File menu and then close the Cyclone window. Your new preset is now finally installed into the Cyclone preset menu. Open up *Twilight II* and test it out!

Fazer!

Fazer! is a *Twilight II* module from Greg Templeman and Eric Shepherd. It started as an algorithm developed to improve graphics compression, but it had the interesting side effect of looking like a pretty good dissolve. Fazer! moves the dots on the screen around in a mathematical pattern that looks pretty random, except that you get striped lines and other interesting effects every few seconds. The dots are repeatedly moved to new locations, until eventually the original screen shows up again.

The use fast-fazer option employs a 62.5K cache to drastically speed up fazing. Double-fazer seems to slow fazing down, but each point is being moved twice as far, so the whole fazing process takes less time overall.

There is also a screen fader built in, which fades between minimum and maximum intensity settings at an adjustable speed. By selecting brightness only, you can turn off "fazing" so only the fader is used almost like another whole module!

The quit after one checkbox causes Fazer! to quit to the next module when in random mode. If you have brightness only selected, the screen brightness will be dimmed to the minimum setting, then intensified to the maximum setting, and then the next module will be run. (So, if you selected Fazer!, brightness only, and Tiler in random mode, if Fazer! was run first, it would dim down the screen and then Tiler would operate on the partially dimmed screen.)

If brightness only is not selected, then Fazer! will quit to the next module after one complete fazing of the screen (i.e. the original screen is arrived at again). Note that while the visual fazing appears very rapid, the entire screen must be fazed over 14,000 times to get back to the original image (over 7,000 times for double-fazer) which takes 30 to 42 minutes on a 10 MHz Apple IIGS.

Movie Theater

Movie Theater allows you to display *PaintWorks* (file type $C2) type animation files when it's time to blank. This popular file format can be viewed and created with programs such as *DreamGrafix*, *PaintWorks*, and *Platinum Paint*. Be careful to select animations that modify the contents of the screen enough to prevent burn-in.

The *T2.SpinLogo.SEA* file on the Extras disk includes a bonus *PaintWorks*-type ($C2) animation for use with the Movie Theater module. This animation is in the form of a self-extracting archive. To install the spinning animation, run the *T2.SpinLogo.SEA* file and select the folder you want the animation to be put in.

Phantom

Phantom lets you use all effects from the Phantasm screen saver (part of *Signature GS*) with *Twilight II*. Phantasm effect modules have a file type of "GS/OS Shell application" ($B5, or EXE). Included with *Twilight II* are a variety of freeware effect modules you can use with Phantom. (All Phantom effect files installed by the procedure outlined previously in the section "Installing *Twilight II*" are installed in a folder named *Phantom.Effects*, in the *Twilight* module folder.)

The setup screen for Phantom has three controls: demo, configure, and select effect. Before blanking with Phantom or using demo or configure, you should select an effect to use by clicking the select effect button or pressing *Command-E*. 'Open' the effect you want to use. Be sure you are selecting a valid effect! Then click save to save the selected effect. Most Phantom effects do not support configure, so if you click it and nothing happens, do not be alarmed. To preview effects, we recommend you use test (or blank now) rather than demo, because some modules may not demo correctly.

Using Signature GS v1.0.2 Effects with Phantom

It has been brought to our attention that for *Signature GS* v1.0.2, Q Labs decided to pre-install their seven effects. This means that our

Signature Phantasm Effect installation script will not work with the *Signature GS* effects if you only have *Signature GS* v1.0.2. This is not a bug in Phantom – all Phantasm effects can be used with Phantom, in their uninstalled form.

Problems with Public Domain Phantom Effects

Some users have reported erratic problems with the public domain Phantom effects (installed into the *Phantom.Effects* folder) included with *Twilight II*. The problem appears to be with the Phantom effects and not with *Twilight II* or the Phantom module. If you notice problems with any of these public domain effects, stop using them – their quality really cannot compete with most of the *Twilight II* modules, and they were included primarily as a bonus.

Sharks and Fish

The "Sharks and Fish" module, by Nathan Mates, is based on the Computer Recreations article from A.K Dewdney in the December 1984 issue of Scientific American (pp. 8-22). Sharks and Fish is a program that simulates to actions of two populations, predator and prey, shark and fish, on a small scale. Each shark must eat a fish at certain limits of time, or it will starve to death. The fish are content to merely swim around, reproducing as they do.

On each unit of time, the fish can move one square up, down, left, or right, if there is space, and breed if it is time to do so. Breeding is simulated by the movement of one of the offspring to a nearby square, while the parents stay in the original square.

Sharks, being predators, are always looking for food. If there is a hapless fish nearby, it will be eaten. Otherwise, the shark will move about, just like a fish. Each shark must eat every so often, or it will starve and die.

Although the world size is fixed, there are a number of parameters that can be set from this module's setup window. In increments of 20, you can change the initial number of fish, the number of sharks in increments of 10, and the base characteristics of the sharks and the fish. For the breeding and starving times, the number is the number of cycles before that action passes. Thus, a breeding of one means that offspring will be born every turn, if there is room for them. Likewise, a starving of one means that the sharks will starve every tum, so they will all die off in a tum.

Sharks and Fish can be interesting to watch and play with – it also forms a cool screen saver. The graphics were optimized for the starting light-blue world, but the blue can potentially burn into the monitor if it is left going for an overly excessive period of time.

Therefore, the option to allow color cycling (changing the colors of the world slightly every tum) is available, and should be use if Sharks and Fish is used as a frequent screen saver.

S.L.E.D.

S.L.E.D. uses its own scripting language to allow you to control exactly what is displayed on the virtual LED sign. The scripts are saved as ordinary Text of Teach files in the "SLED.Messages" directory within the Twilight folder. Any text you put in the script will be scrolled across the display from right to left with the default red color. Using the scripting language you can be really fancy and add wipes, fades, colors, and many other special effects.

There are many advanced effects, including QIX, Lasers, as well as an Easter egg invoked if you press Caps Lock and then Control. Full details of script commands can be found on the Call-A.P.P.L.E. GitHub page: https://github.com/callapple

YouDrawIt!

The YouDrawIt module allows you to use any Apple IIGS paint program to design graphics that will be animated when the screen is blanked. Enclosed on the *Twilight II* disk are what we feel represent the best assortment of animations previously drawn by users like yourself. Use them for ideas and examples. (During the installation procedure, these files are copied into a folder named *YDI.Animations* in the *Twilight* module folder.)

There are two types of animation picture files for use with YouDrawIt: normal animation template files (ATF's), and extended animation template files (EATF's.) The only difference is that ATF's allow 14 frames of animation and EATF's allow 28. (Because of this, EATF's can also take up twice as much space on disk.) These are standard Apple Preferred Format (APF) pictures – make sure you tell your paint program to save ATF's/EATF's in APF format for use with YouDrawIt. We recommend you use a nomenclature of giving the filenames of ATF's a suffix of ".ATF" and the filenames of EATF's a suffix of ".EATF" to prevent confusion.

To set the animation that will be used when it is time for YouDrawIt to blank the screen, click the set animation path button on the YouDrawIt setup screen, or press *Command-A*. Then 'open' the animation file that you want to use. ATF/EATF files can be located on any disk, with one restriction – they must be on a disk present when YouDrawIt blanks the screen. If YouDrawIt can't find the currently selected ATF / EATF, you will get an error. This won't hurt anything, but an error message is a lot less interesting to watch!

Creating your own animations for use with YouDrawIt is a fun and enjoyable experience. Blank versions of these picture templates are included with *Twilight II*. They have filenames of *Blank.ATF* and *Blank.EATF*. To create your own animation, do the following:

1. Load up either of these blank templates into your favorite paint program.

2. Draw each frame in the boxes provided.

3. Fill in the box (using the paint bucket tool) next to the number of frames in your file. You may fill it with any color other than the color that was there to begin with.

You can now select the picture file from YouDrawIt. When the screen is blanked, your animation will be run. Other modules have images which can be customized as well, such as Fish, Globe, and Toast. See the sample images for an example.

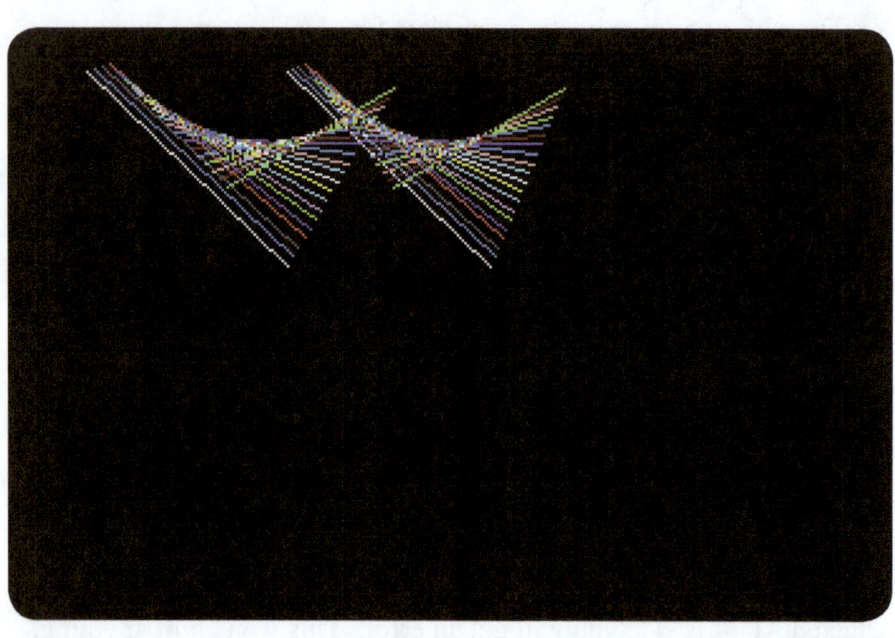

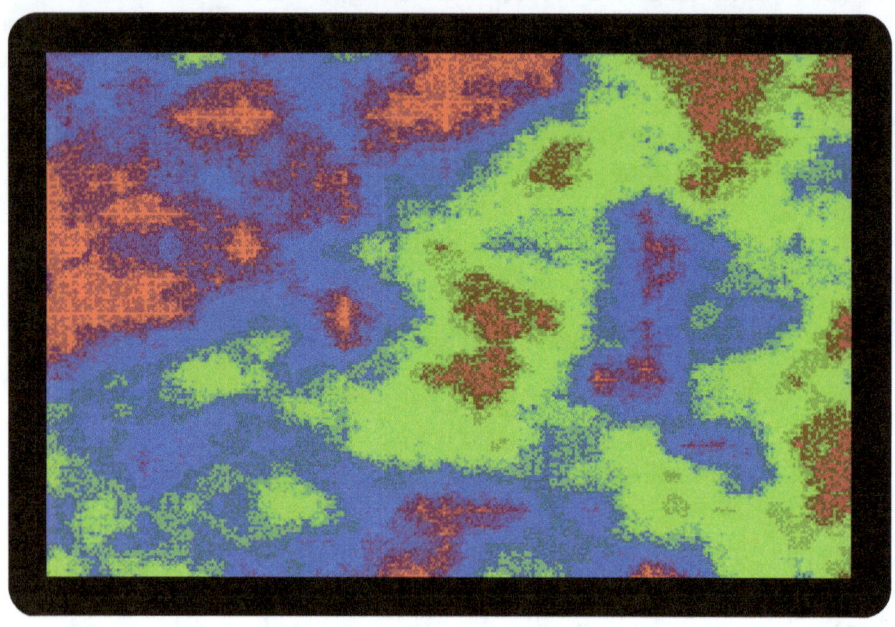

OTHER INFORMATION

This section contains miscellaneous features, tips, and hints not found elsewhere in this manual.

Temporary Deactivation

To temporarily deactivate *Twilight II* at any time after loading, press and hold down Shift and Clear until the border color flashes. *Twilight II's* overhead will then be minimized and the screen will not blank, but no memory will be freed. (To free memory after loading you must purge *Twilight II*.) If you press Shift-Clear again, you can toggle *Twilight II* back on. The border will flash a different color to inform you that *Twilight II* is being reactivated. The colors the border will flash will depend on what color your border normally is.

The status of this option is also reflected by the *Twilight II* active control on the main window and is not saved to disk.

Restoring Default Settings

If for some reason you should ever want to restore *Twilight II* to its default settings, simply delete the Twilight.Setup file (located in the Twilight folder.)

Control-Booting

You can force *Twilight II* not to install itself by holding down Control while the computer is being started. To denote this, a red X will be drawn over the *Twilight II* icon when it is displayed at the bottom of the screen. This feature will only work when you have *Twilight II* installed in the CDevs folder of your startup disk. For control-booting to work, Control must be the only key held down during startup, and you must hold it down before *Twilight II* loads.

Modules with Sound Effects

Due to the architecture of the IIGS, it is not always possible for some modules (e.g. Fireworks) to always play their digitized sound effects. Whether the sounds play or not depends on what program you are currently running, in the same way that system sounds configured with the Sound control panel do not play all the time.

Disabled Modules

Any *Twilight II* module can be made inactive with a utility such as the Finder. After a module has been made inactive, it will not appear in the main window's available module list in any way. Since the more modules you have installed, the longer it takes each time to open up *Twilight II*, disabling infrequently used modules can save time. The icons of disabled *Twilight II* modules have a red X drawn over them so they are easily distinguishable from the Finder. In future versions of *Twilight II*, we plan to speed up the time it takes to open the main window.

Module Limits

All versions of *Twilight II* version 1.1 and newer can handle any amount of modules limited only by available memory and disk space (and patience.)

Random Mode Special Behavior

Some modules have special features or behave differently in random mode. Modules such as *Headlines*, *Mountains*, S*tring Art*, and *Plasma* have options to quit to the next module after one headline, mountain, string art, or plasma screen has been generated (in random mode only). *Short Out* and *Color by Color* will automatically quit to the next module when run from random mode with more than one module selected. *Meltdown* will quit to the next module after a few minutes in random mode instead of flipping the screen upside down.

You can combine these options for some really neat effects! Here are some ideas of ours that you can try in random mode. You must have the 'in random mode, quit after one...' option turned on in all modules involved, where it is available. These are just a few examples – the possibilities are endless!

- Select Short Out with any other module. If Short Out comes up first, it will short the screen out and then run the next module. For instance, select Short Out with String Art. After one string art has been completed, the screen will short out and another string art will be created.

- Select Mountains with the Color by Color module. After one mountain screen has been generated, the screen will fade out, color by color. After all the colors have faded out, another mountain scene will be rendered!

- Select Plasma and Worms. If *Twilight II* runs Plasma first, one plasma screen will be drawn, and then worms will draw over the plasma.

Fazer! adds even more possibilities to this list! When "brightness only" and "quit after one" are set, Fazer! will dim the screen to the intensity you specify and then the next module will be run. For instance, the screen can be faded out part way before a module such as Tiler or Worms is run. The combinations are endless!

Delayed Blanking During Printing

When the screen blanks during printing you may experience a several second delay before the screen is blanked, and before it is restored.

Blanking in ProDOS 8 Programs

The screen is always background blanked in ProDOS 8 programs, unless ProDOS 8 blanking is turned off via the text screen blank option (in Setup: Options), or *Twilight II* is deactivated.

Preventing Burn In

During the beta test cycle, a few people raised concerns that some of the modules included with *Twilight II* may not prevent burn in as well as others. We feel this warrants further discussion.

Protecting against burn-in seems to be somewhat of a problem with every modular screen saver, to some extent – modules put stuff on the screen, and that blanked image may still wind up burned in (although it won't happen nearly as quickly). Although *Twilight II* as a whole has been tested extensively to prevent screen burn in and the modules have been designed to avoid burn in, there is always the possibility that other modules or animations may be prone to not protecting the screen as well as others. Under normal use this will probably never be noticeable.

Some modules can be set up for better protection. For example, Snow will protect your monitor better when told to clear the screen after a short period of time. The user can help this situation by choosing a balance of protective modules and options. A good effect module will frequently change the intensities and/or positions of images onscreen.

Bum-in problems occur from pixels being continually stimulated at relatively high intensities. These problems are more prone to occur when pixels are left unchanged for a long period of time or are frequently returned to their original color in a small amount of time. Normal intensity text and menu bars are usually unchanging images with potentially damaging high intensity. However, if a pixel is stimulated at half the intensity, it will take twice as long, or longer, to burn. Also, remember that one pixel isn't really what one should be concerned with. On color monitors, there are three phosphors per pixel. Each phosphor dot must be considered.

For example, Scanner projects a relatively narrow full intensity band, bordered by progressively lower intensity lines. The high intensity part is over any particular part of the screen for only about 17% of the time, and the same goes for the rest of it. Now, if we say that the phosphors will burn-in in exact proportion to how long they're lit, not counting intensity, then you're looking at 83% less burning than if it was on continually. What this means is that one would have to leave scanner running for an outrageous and unreasonable long amount of time for anything bad to happen.

While we have done extensive testing to avoid any form of burn in, there is always the remote possibility that it could happen, especially if a mediocre module is left on screen for several days. We regret that we cannot take any responsibility if burn-in does occur. It is up to the user to responsibly decide which modules and options should be used with caution, but hopefully a future version of *Twilight II* we will have an option to automatically switch modules after so many minutes.

Twilight II and *Express* from Seven Hills Software

If Express is transparently spooling to the printer in the background, and the screen foreground blanks, the printing will stop until the screen un-blanks. While not truly at fault, Seven Hills can make a very minor change in their code to fix this slight inconvenience. They will judge the amount of calls they receive and if it looks like this fix can't wait until a future "significant" update, release of an interim version that forces background blanking during background printing (i.e. *Twilight II* would make the screen black automatically whenever something is printing in the background) is a definite possibility.

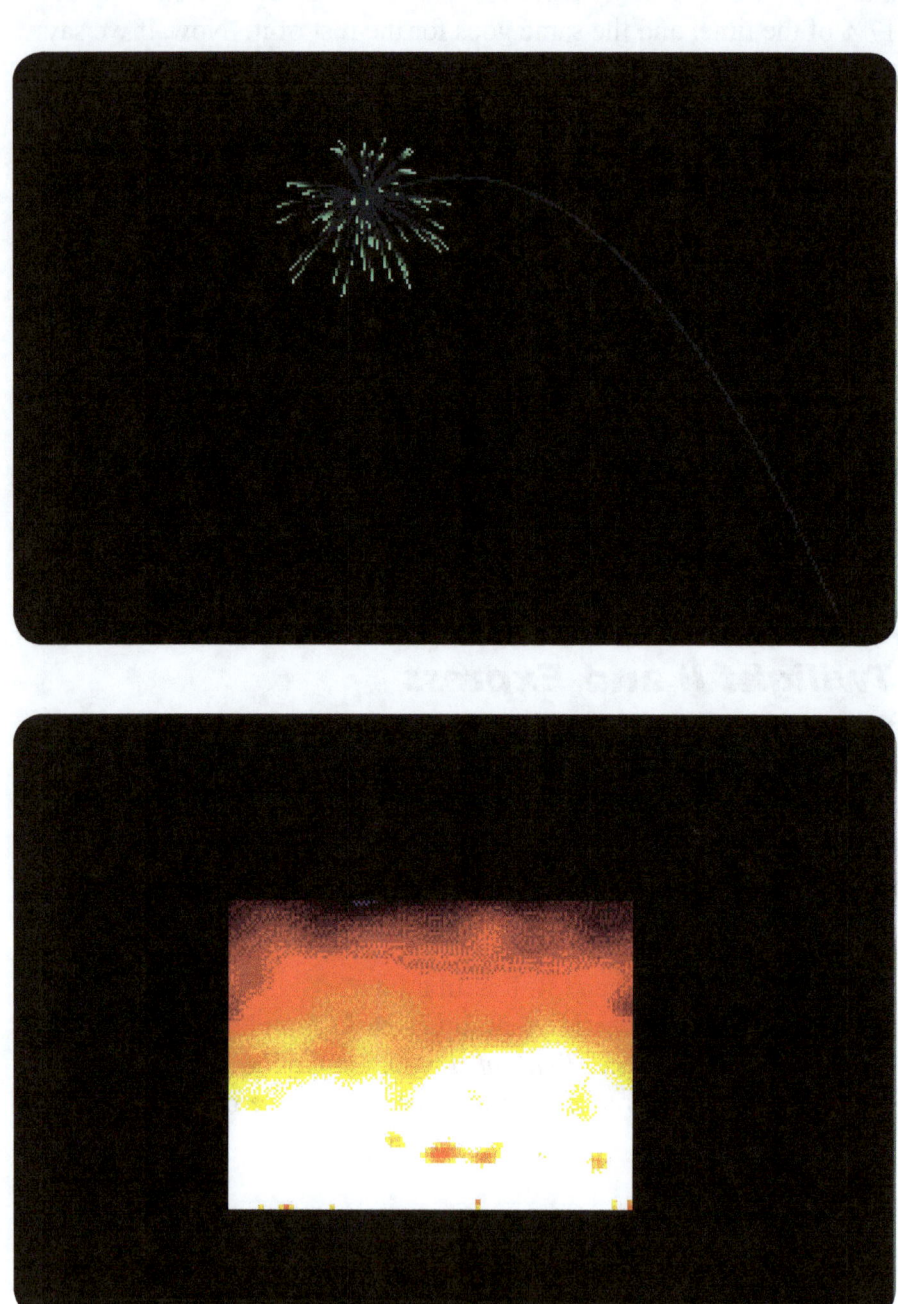

APPENDIX I

Common Questions and Answers

I'm in a GS/OS desktop-based program, and the screen won't blank while the program is busy.

Twilight II does everything possible to blank the screen in as many programs as possible. However, due to the design of certain programs and the architecture of the Apple IIGS, *Twilight II* is unable to blank or animate the screen in all programs all the time.

A general rule of thumb, true most of the time, is if you are able to in some way interact with the program you are running, the screen will be able to blank. For instance, the screen can be blanked during printing because you can always cancel the printing with *Command-Period*, the screen is able to be blanked during copying files with the Finder because you can click the cancel button to stop the copy.

The screen can be blanked in the middle of programs such as *AppleWorks GS* and *GraphicWriter III* because you can select something from a menu or type a key that the program will recognize. Whenever the desktop program running will recognize your input, *Twilight II* will usually be able to blank the screen. (Note that in text mode-based programs, the screen is always able to be blanked at virtually any time.)

Programmers are encouraged to follow a few simple guidelines to allow the fullest compatibility with *Twilight II*, so the desktop screen can always be blanked. See "Writing *Twilight II* Savvy Programs" in Appendix II for more information.

Twilight II will never blank on its own – I must always move to a blank now corner. After installing Twilight II, my computer sometimes crashes or hangs.

Several different things amid be happening. For some reason, the *Twilight.Setup* file could have been corrupted. This might have happened for a number of reasons, such as if you turned off the computer or press *Command-Control-Reset* to reboot while the *Twilight II* main window was open – be sure to always close *Twilight II* first! In this case, you should try deleting *Twilight.Setup* (which is created in the *Twilight* module folder, or your user folder if you are on an AppleShare network) and rebooting. (Note that all your saved setup will be lost and must be reset to your preferences.)

Another possibility could be that there is a conflict between *Twilight II* and another one of your installed INITs, Desk Accessories (DA's), or Control Panels (CDevs). We have tried to minimize and correct all such incompatibilities as possible, but nonetheless some may still exist.

To see if there is a conflict, try starting your computer with Apple's self-booting *System Disk* that is a part of System 6. This disk will only have Apple's programs installed. When the Finder comes up, locate the *Twilight.II* control panel icon and double-click it to install it. If the screen will now blank on its own, then you definitely have a conflict between *Twilight II* and an INIT, DA, or Control Panel. The next step is to locate which file is conflicting. To determine this, try deactivating each of your INITS, DA's, and Control Panels one at a time and then rebooting. Eventually you will find the one conflicting with *Twilight II*.

If you suspect that *Twilight II* is conflicting with a specific program or init, you can control-boot (by holding down control during startup) to stop *Twilight II* from installing into memory, to see if your suspicions are correct. If you notice *Twilight II* inhibiting any other programs from working properly, be sure to report this to us so we can work at fixing the problems or creating workarounds.

After Twilight II background blanks during printing, why does my printout turn all black?

A few older, somewhat poorly written, GS/OS printer drivers make certain assumptions about the state of the computer during printing. If you are using one of these drivers, you have several options:

- Change the WatchCursor feature (in *Setup: Options*) to 'don't blank'.

- Always move the mouse to a never blank corner before printing.

- Turn on caps lock "lock" (in *Setup: Options*) and press *Caps Lock* before printing, deactivate or purge *Twilight II* before printing and reactivate or reinstall after the printing is done update your printer driver. All drivers from Independence and Harmonie will work fine, and Apple is in the process of fixing theirs hopefully for System 6.0.1.

When the Twilight II icon appears during startup, the computer beeps and then the icon is crossed out.

Twilight II has encountered a serious error while starting up. Because the error occurred during boot, *Twilight II* has no way to tell you what happened, so installation and activation are skipped. If you would like a more descriptive error message, double-click the Twilight.II icon from the Finder.

Twilight II can often be restored to working order by deleting the *Twilight.Setup* file in the *Twilight* folder. This will fix many situations but is not a cure-all. Also make sure the disk *Twilight II* is on is not write protected. If none of these suggestions nor the error message help, try reinstalling *Twilight II*. If that does not help, contact us.

When I run my telecommunication program with Twilight II installed, some of incoming characters are lost.

Twilight II 1.0 and 1.1 were not as well behaved in this regard as this current version of *Twilight II*. If you are using *Spectrum* 2.x, then use the *Twilight II* XCMD included with it (or the XCMD distributed as part of this package) to turn *Twilight II* off either whenever *Spectrum* is online, or when it is running.

After installing the new XCMD included in this *Twilight II* distribution, the options will be available from the Xtras/Options (or Xtras/File Transfer Options) menu.

If you choose not to install the new XCMD, you can open an Editor Window (Command-E), type this as the first line in the file:

```
external TwilightII
```

and press Command-'-' (command and the minus key just left of the zero key). It is recommended that you choose to "Inactivate Twilight II while using Spectrum" for the best performance.

Twilight II's WatchCursor option does not work in one of my programs.

This option (having *Twilight II* automatically background blank or never blank when the cursor on-screen is a watch) only works with programs that use the standard method of displaying a watch. Fortunately, the majority of all programs work just fine. However, there are a few programs that insist on displaying a watch in a nonstandard way (e.g. *GraphicWriter III* and *HyperCard IIGS*).

Unfortunately, there is no way for you to make these programs work with *Twilight II's* Watch Cursor option. If this disturbs you, we encourage you to contact the publishers of programs such as these and tell them you'd like to see them fixed.

What does "Unknown Error $0120" mean?

The Control Panels window occasionally gives this error if there is a severe RAM shortage. Try freeing up some memory.

What does "Error $0201" mean?

In general, this is an out of memory error. If this happens when launching a ProDOS 8 application, this tends to mean that some program as forgotten to release memory allocated in the first 128K of RAM, which is required for ProDOS 8 stuff. Some reports have come up that 0201s may occur on their system after using Setup a lot from within UtilityLaunch, but this has been unable to be replicated well enough to find and fix any possible bug in either Twilight II or UL.

Some modules aren't using TrueType fonts.

(The commercial software "Pointless" by WestCode software is required for a IIGS to use Truetype fonts at all.)

Certain modules like Fading Clock and Headlines allow you to specify what font you wish to have things displayed with. It has been noticed that if a TrueType-only font and size (i.e. no bitmap exists for that size) is selected, it will occasionally be drawn as an ugly scaled up 'Shaston' (IIGS default font) versus the expected TT font. After a few requests for the font, Pointless may give the module a nice font as expected.

This appears to be a bug in Pointless, and has not been investigated further as it is only the occasional graphical quirk. Select a font and size for which you have a bitmap if you don't want to be bothered by this. Pointless can render off a font in the style and size you want if desired – see its Control Panel menu.

Cool Cursor Control Panel is forcing background blanks or causing other problems.

Various versions of the Cool Cursor Control Panel (from *GS+ Magazine* v5n3) could do various things with *Twilight II*, such as forcing a background blank of *Twilight II* during printing, even if the Twilight II setup has the wait cursor set to "Don't Blank." *Twilight II* honors requests from other programs over the setup, sorry.

APPENDIX II

TECHNICAL INFORMATION

This section is intended to provide information on how to modify, understand, or take advantage of the more technical aspects of *Twilight II*. This section is mainly intended for programmers, but some information might be of general interest.

Useful Resources

There are three resources (in *Twilight II's* resource fork) that would be worth modifying with a resource editor, such as *Foundation* from Lunar Productions.

rWString($00000001)

This resource contains the name of the directory that *Twilight II* will look for modules in. Normally it is set to "Twilight" but it can be set to any valid name you like.

rWString($00000002)

The filename *Twilight II* stores its preferences in is contained in this resource. Normally this is "Twilight.Setup."

$0001($00000001)

This resource, one word in size, contains an integer value controlling how many modules *Twilight II* can handle. It is currently preset to 50 to save memory, but if you should install more modules than this, you must change this resource or only the first 40 will be recognized. After modifying this resource, you must delete *Twilight.Setup* for the change to take effect.

Writing *Twilight II* Savvy Programs

Via GS/OS System 6's new inter-process communication (IPC) capabilities, *Twilight II* and other programs can coordinate efforts by communicating with each other. *Twilight II* sports a comprehensive set of routines that inform programs when the screen is blanking and un-blanking and also allow applications to control certain aspects of *Twilight II*.

By following a few simple guidelines (most of which are wisely recommended by Apple), you can insure full compatibility with *Twilight II*. Many of these suggestions will make your programs much more friendly to the system as a whole, and to other programs as well. This results in a much more pleasant computing experience for the user.

General Guidelines

Desktop Programs

Twilight II can only blank the screen in the desktop environment when QuickDraw II and the Event Manager are started, and `SystemTask`, `GetNextEvent`, or `TaskMaster` is called. Keep this in mind if you want *Twilight II* to be able to blank in your program.

If your program is doing something that should not be interrupted (e.g. unshrinking files, copying files, etc.), you have several options. If you call `WaitCursor` and then periodically call `SystemTask`, `GetNextEvent`, or `TaskMaster`, then *Twilight II* will be able to step in and background blank the screen (if the appropriate WatchCursor option is set) and let your program keep running. If at any time you think the screen must be blanked in the background, then you can use the `t2ForceBkgBlank` IPC request. If the screen should not be blanked at all, you can turn *Twilight II* off and on at will.

Also, if your program does not use the standard watch cursor (by calling the toolbox `WaitCursor` call) to indicate the computer is working (such as Foundation's spinning moon, the spinning beach ball of *AppleWorks GS*, and GS+'s *Cool Cursor* control panel, or just a custom watch image as *GraphicWriter III* and *HyperCard IIGS*), you also should also use the `t2ForceBkgBlank` IPC request before and after displaying your custom cursor or cursor animation. This will allow the WatchCursor features to work with your program.

Finally, whenever you need to hide and show the menu bar, you should only use the `HideMenuBar` and `ShowMenuBar` tool calls.

Tips

Usually it is not a good idea to install an interrupt that modifies the palettes. When *Twilight II* kicks in, it has no way to stop your interrupts, so the screen could get pretty nasty looking.

If you must patch the tool dispatcher vector, make sure you do it in the way described in Apple IIGS technote #87. Otherwise, the purge *Twilight II* option will not function properly.

If you ever need to get or set the super high-resolution palettes, use the appropriate QuickDraw II call. Do not access the palettes directly, or you will cause conflicts with background blanking.

If you always want to be informed when *Twilight II* blanks the text screen, do not overuse the scheduler. For if the scheduler task queue is full when the text screen blanks, you never will be notified of the blank.

Twilight II IPC Routines

We feel that *Twilight II* and your program should work together, not against each other. *Twilight II* will notify your program when it is blanking the screen, and in some cases you will even be given the option to abort the blank. Your program can control many aspects of *Twilight II's* operation through the *Twilight II* IPC routines.

Writing *Twilight II* Modules

Twilight II employs an advanced custom module format, very similar to CDevs. *Twilight II* modules can be written in assembly language, C, Pascal, or any combination of the three, and have file type $BC (generic load file) and auxiliary type $4004. The modules included with *Twilight II* have been written in assembly and C. *Twilight II* itself was written in 100% assembly language. Writing *Twilight II* modules can be a very fun and satisfying task.

Appendix III

Generation 2 Module Format

The Generation 2 Module Format (G2MF) represents a vast change from the way modules were previously called.

Twilight I v1.0 brought a very simple module format (see the *Twilight I* developer kit for more information.) But along with that simplicity was lack of power, and lack of expansion ability. The G2MF, as implemented in *Twilight II*, represents a vast step forward. It has been designed with all the present and potential future needs in mind. Old modules are not directly compatible and need to be recompiled.

At all times, try to keep your module changing the screen enough to prevent burn in! Use some discretion on this issue. When modules are automatically switched after a given amount of time, hopefully your module won't have to worry so much about protecting the screen (since the next module will probably change the screen in a different way).

In addition to the documentation contained within this document, please note that we also have provided sample module source code in C, *Orca/M* assembly, and *Merlin* assembly.

We have added some IPC requests that modules can use to make modules featuring setup easier to write. The "IPC Module Command" documentation is on page 95.

Twilight II Module File Format

A *Twilight II* module is defined by a file with filetype $BC (Generic Load File – GLF) auxtype $4004 (suggested abbreviation: T2M) with a data fork containing a routine capable of handling at least a `BlankT2` message, and a resource fork containing a minimum of the following:

Resource Type	Resource ID	Description
rLETextBox2 ($800B)	$0010DD01	Module specific message to be printed in the "About Module" dialog box.
rIcon ($8001)	$0010DD01	Module specific icon to be displayed in the "About Module" dialog box.
rVersion ($8029)	$00000001	Version resource for the module.
rT2ModuleFlags ($D001)	$0000001	Special resource similar to `rCDevFlags` in concept.

In addition, it is recommended the following are also present:

rComment ($802A)	$00000001	Comment for the user, for Finder 6.0.
rComment ($802A)	$00000002	Message to tell the user to access modules thru T2, not by double-click.

The about module window may eventually display your about LETextBox2 string in a textEdit control, so be prepared for this.

The Rez definition for the format of `rT2ModuleFlags` is as follows:

```
type rT2ModuleFlags {
      byte = $01;             /* module flags version - use 1 */
      hex unsigned word;      /* module flags word */
      byte;                   /* enabled flag (unimplemented) */
      hex unsigned word;      /* minimum T2 version required */
      hex unsigned word;      /* reserved */
      pstring[25];            /* module name */
};
```

Currently, these bits of the flag word of rT2ModuleFlags are defined
and implemented:

Bit 0 ($0001)   fSetup

The module supports setup. The module must be capable of receiving
and doing something specific for MakeT2, SaveT2, LoadSetupT2,
and HitT2 (minimum.)

Bit 1 ($0002)   fFadeOut

The module wants the previous screen to fade out before receiving
a BlankT2 message. After fading out, the SCBs, palettes, and pixel
data will be set to NIL. There is no need for you to re-zero them if you
have this bit set!

Bit 2 ($0004)   fFadein

The module wants the saved screen to fade in after returning from a
BlankT2 message.

Bit 3 ($0008)   fGrafPort320

This bit when set tells *Twilight II* to open a new port and then set all
the SCBs to 320 mode before calling BlankT2. *Twilight II* will save
the old port, open up a new port, set the current port to the new port,
and then set all the SCBs to use palette $0, 320 mode, and then will set
the LocInfo of the new port to have a bounds of (0,0,200,320) and a
visRgn of the same size.

Bit 4 ($0010)   fGrafPort640

This bit when set tells *Twilight II* to open a new port and then set all the SCBs to 640 mode before calling `BlankT2`. *Twilight II* will save the old port, open up a new port, set the current port to the new port, and then set all the SCBs to use palette $0, 640 mode, and then will set the `LocInfo` of the new port to have a bounds of (0,0,200,640) and a `visRgn` of the same size.

Bit 5 ($0020)   fLoadSetupBoot

`LoadSetupT2` will be called right after the module is loaded (either at boot time, or when the CDev window is being closed), and `UnloadSetupT2` will be called only right before your module is being disposed of.

Bit 6 ($0040)   fLoadSetupBlank

`LoadSetupT2` will be called right before `BlankT2`, and `UnloadSetupT2` will be called right after `BlankT2`, not when the module has been just loaded.

Bit 7 ($0080)   fOpenRForkWriteEnabled

Open the module's resource fork with read and write access instead of normal read access only before sending `MakeT2`. This bit is for special circumstances only. Usage is strongly discouraged whenever possible.

Bit 8 ($0100)   fMostCommonPalette

Have *Twilight II* take a tally of which lines use which palette, and set all the SCBs to use the most commonly used palette.

Bit 9 ($0200)   fReqUsableScreen

The module requires a "usable" screen. (See discussion below.)

Bit 10 ($0400)   fLeavesUsableScreen

The module leaves a "usable" screen.

Bit 11 ($0800)   fLeavesCycleScreen

The module leaves a screen which can be color cycled by the next module, where applicable. NOTE: this is not implemented in *Twilight II* v2.

Bit 12 ($1000)   fPrematureExit

The module always exits before move:Ptr becomes true, when in random mode (e.g. Short Out, Color by Color.) This feature is not implemented in Twilight II v2, but is present to make switching modules after so many minutes much better in the future!

The minimum *Twilight II* version word of `T2ModuleFlags` is BCD, in the same format as toolbox version words in Apple IIGS Technote 100. For example, $0101 represents *Twilight II* version 1.0.1. If the version of *Twilight II* is not great enough, *Twilight II* will display the module as dimmed. If the version of the rT2ModuleFlags resource is incorrect (i.e. not $01) or the *Twilight II* module has been inactivated (given an auxtype of $C004), then the module will not be displayed at all.

In addition, it should be noted that modules are free to put whatever else they want in their resource forks. Please put your setup controls in your resource fork if your module supports setup. Please use our defined resource types (i.e. `rT2ModuleWord`, `rByteArray`, etc.), where applicable, for consistency. Also, we suggest that you put as much of your data in resources as possible, for three reasons:

1. Your module's data doesn't have to stay around in memory all the time, using valuable memory space (instead it can be loaded in `LoadSetupT2`, which can be called right before your module is called for super-memory-efficiency)

2. The advanced user can use a resource editor to modify your module data if necessary.

3. Resources should be used whenever and wherever possible because of the flexibility they offer.

Twilight II Module Messages

Twilight II modules are now sent "messages" to perform certain actions in the same way the Control Panel NDA sends action event codes to CDevs. (As a side effect, this makes modules a lot easier to write in "C" for you can just define them as CDevs for practical purposes – see the Orca/C sample module source for more information!)

Currently there are seven defined action types. The only one modules are required to support is `BlankT2`. Support of the rest is optional, but recommended.

At any time, your module may call `MMStartUp` to get the ID it is running under. The ID returned from `MMStartUp` is what the data fork of the module was loaded with using the System Loader, so it is advisable to first create a few new modified auxID's to allocate all your memory with. Create as many auxID's as you wish, and do whatever you want with them, just don't delete the id returned from MMStartUp and don't use it to allocate extra memory.

When the data fork of a module is called and sent an action message, the stack is set up like this:

INPUTS:

```
|previous contents|
+-----------------+
|     T2Result    | Long - Result space.
+-----------------+
|     T2Message   | Word - Action to perform.
+-----------------+
|     T2data1     | Long - Action specific input.
+-----------------+
|     T2data2     | Long - Action specific input.
+-----------------+
|     rtlAddr     | 3 bytes - Return address.
+-----------------+
```

The module must return control to *Twilight II* with the stack arranged as follows:

OUTPUTS:

```
|previous contents|
+-----------------+
|      T2Result   | Long - Action specific output.
+-----------------+
|      rtlAddr    | 3 bytes - Return address.
+-----------------+
```

Message 0: MakeT2

This message is sent only to modules which support setup, as indicated by their `T2ModuleFlags` resource. A `MakeT2` message is sent when the module's menu item is selected from the setup popup control in the setup window. It tells the module to create its setup-specific controls in the setup window. When the user selects the popup menu item for setup for your module, *Twilight II* loads the data fork of your module into memory (again if necessary) and calls `MakeT2`. It is the module's responsibility to position its controls below the setup window's pseudo-info bar.

Your module must return in `T2Result` (lo) the highest control ID (not resource ID!) of the controls it just created. This means that you must start numbering your control IDs with 1, going consecutively through the highest ID that must be returned in `T2Result` (lo). This highest ID number will be used by *Twilight II* when it is time to erase and dispose of the controls.

If you need to load the last saved setup configuration values of your module so you can set up your controls to reflect the current status of these flags, you must save the current resource file, set the current resource file to `T2Data2` (lo), read in or create, if necessary, your configuration flag resources, then restore the original resource file (probably that of your own module's resource fork.) Again, see our sample source if this sounds confusing.

(You can create your config resources from scratch at either `MakeT2` or `SaveT2`; we recommend making new setup resources-if they don't already exist-during `SaveT2`.) You must create your setup resources the first time the user configures your module after installation or after deleting `Twilight.Setup`. The resource search path should be preset by Twilight II to:

`«Your Module»,Twilight.II,ControlPanel,Sys.Resources.`

Modules are free to use TextEdit controls in their setup dialogs without any problems or extra effort. Try to take care that the setup window may enlarge in the future when designing your control layout.

Just for your information, the horizontal line control always present in the setup window has QuickDraw II coordinates of (20,0,21,350).

All direct page space is reserved for use by *Twilight II*. The following parameters are passed on the stack:

`T2Message`	=	MakeT2 ($0000.)
`T2Data1`	=	Window pointer of the setup modeless window.
`T2Data2` (hi)	=	Reserved (do not modify!)
`T2Data2` (lo)	=	Resource file ID of the opened resource fork of `Twilight.Setup`.
`T2Result` (hi)	=	Reserved (do *not* modify!)
`T2Result` (lo)	=	Highest control ID of module specific setup controls.

Control IDs in the range $07FEFFE0 through $07FEFFFF are currently reserved for use by the CDev and should not be used by modules.

Message 1: SaveT2

A `SaveT2` message is passed to your module when your module is presently being configured, and the user clicks on the "update" control in the pseudo-info bar. Saving new configuration data was implemented in this fashion so that the user can choose not to save the new settings if a mistake is made somewhere. Typically in your `SaveT2` handler you will first set the current resource file to `Twilight.Setup`, and then you will load in any existing configuration resources specific to your module and modify them

to reflect the user's new changes. Don't forget to handle a first-case
scenario – the resources may not be there if your module was never
configured before, so you might have to create them and then store
the new values the user just chose. (See "Twilight.Setup" section
below.) All parameters are reserved, but ones passed with MakeT2
are still valid for use. All direct page space is also reserved for use by
Twilight II.

T2Message	=	SaveT2 ($0001.)
T2Data1	=	Reserved (do *not* modify!)
T2Data2	=	Reserved (do *not* modify!)
T2Result	=	Reserved (do *not* modify!)

Message 2: BlankT2

BlankT2 is the one message modules are required to support.
Modules are provided with a direct page of their own to be used in
any manner. Do whatever you need to animate the screen! Note that
the resource search path is undefined, and usually should be left that
way (i.e. in most cases you should not be loading any resources in the
BlankT2 handler!) Please see the special section "Special Notes on
When Resources Are and Should Be Loaded" under "Setup Resources"
for if your module has a valid reason to be loading data resources
from your own resource fork during BlankT2 and not during
LoadSetupT2.

Remember, that if you set the appropriate T2ModuleFlags bits,
the screen might be already faded out when your BlankT2 handler
gets control. *Twilight II* will automatically preserve and restore
the user's original border color for you and set the current color to
black. *Twilight II* will also always open a new GrafPort for your use.
T2ModuleFlags bits fGrafPort320 and fGrafPort640 will
govern any special properties of this port. (See description above.)
Otherwise you will just get whatever default port QuickDraw II gave
to *Twilight II* when it called OpenPort.

To ease the creation of modules with high speed advanced animation
effects that require the shadow screen to work their magic, *Twilight II*
does all the work in securing shadow memory for all modules.

Twilight II indicates that it was able to secure the shadowing screen for your module's use by turning on shadowing before calling your module. (So if you're drawing to the SHR screen directly, be sure to check if shadowing is on. If it is, you must use bank $01 SHR, else you must use bank $El SHR. If you're using QuickDraw II exclusively, you don't have to worry about checking which bank to use.) When shadowing is on and your `BlankT2` handler is called, $012000-A000 is guaranteed to be the same as $E12000-A000.

What if your module absolutely *requires* shadowing to function properly? This is okay – it is a tradeoff. What you should do in such a situation is first to check if shadowing is already on. If it is, do your stuff – modify any parts of $012000-A000 and $El2000-A000 and feel free to turn shadowing off and on if you need to for your animation Gust make sure that the value of the `SHADOW` softswitch is the same when your module exits `BlankT2` as when it was first called.) However, if shadowing is not available (indicated by SHR shadowing turned off when your module gets control) you should exit back with an error string that the internal `DrawString` error module can show to the user.

Twilight II will also make sure the Font Manager is started before calling BlankT2.

The state of the system is as follows:

Port = A default new port, or a specific mode (see above.)

Pen/Background Color = Undefined, but pen is hidden for you.
and Pattern

Resource File Path = Undefined. (That set by the bottom application.)

Resource Application = Undefined except when the *Twilight II* main window is open and your module is called by the user moving to a blank now comer. In this case, the resource application is guaranteed to be that of the Control Panel NDA. (This supports modules storing resources that have to be loaded during blank in their own resource fork, using T2ShareMemory so they can be blanked while being configured.)

Module's Resource Fork = Not open and module not logged into Resource Manager, except if the module's setup window is open at the same time of blank.

Color Tables = Table $0 set to default QuickDraw II palette, tables $1 through $F set to black ($000) if fFadeOut was set. If fGrafPort320 or fGrafPort640 is set then table $0 will be set to the default color table. Otherwise palettes are those set by the bottom application.

Current Pixel Data = Screen memory initialized to $00 if fFadeOut was set. Otherwise set to that of the bottom application.

Current Screen Mode = 320 (all SCBs ANDed with $7F) if fGrafPort320 is set, 640 (all SCBs ORed with $80) if fGrafPort640 is set, otherwise set to that of the bottom application.

Border Color = Black.

T2Message = BlankT2 ($0002.)

T2Data1 = Pointer to Boolean movement flag (movePtr) indicating whether the module should return to T2 or not. The following are currently defined values for movePtr; all other values are reserved.

$0000	No movement has occurred; module should remain active unless returning to T2 with an error string.
$0001	The user has interacted with the computer; your module should now return normally to T2.
$0002-FFFE	Reserved.
$FFFF	The module must exit because a specified number of minutes have elapsed in Random Mode, and *Twilight II* is moving onto the next selected random module. NOTE: not implemented in Twilight II v2.

As soon as **movePtr** turns non-zero, the module is required to return to T2. (If Caps Lock "Lock" is on, and caps lock is down, your module can keep running forever, but **movePtr** also will not turn to 1 until caps lock is released.) If you don't return to T2 at least within 2 seconds after **movePtr** has become 1, then be sure you test your module well, as it has the potential to wreck havoc on *Twilight II*.

T2Data2 (hi) = Reserved (do *not* modify!)

T2Data2 (lo) = Bits defined as follows:

bmiBlankNow	$0001	Module is being called from "blank now"
bmiCycleColors	$0002	The previous module left a screen which can be color cycled. NOTE: this is not implemented in Twilight II v2.

T2Result (lo 3 bytes) = Handle to error c-string. If no errors occurred, pass NIL. Otherwise pass a handle (allocated using your memory ID) containing an error string that you'd like T2 to inform the user about. The error string must be a c-string. Up to one carriage return ($0D) may be embedded. This handle is passed to the internal DrawString error module – experiment with appropriate lengths of the string. Keep it as short as possible.

T2Result = Optional flag byte (`BlankFlag`). Bits defined as follows (bmr =blank message result), with the rest reserved:

bmrNextModule $01000000

Skip to the next module. Only set this if you want to exit your module without `movePtr` becoming true. Also make sure that more than one module has been selected. If `movePtr` has become true or only one module is selected or you are being called from "blank now", do not set this.

bmrFadein $02000000

The SHR screen should be faded in after all. You don't have to set this bit if it is already set in the module flags word.

bmrLeavesUsableScreen $04000000

The module has left a "usable" screen after all. You don't have to set this bit if it is already set in the module flags word.

bmrLeavesCycleScreen $08000000

The module has left a screen which can be color cycled after all. You don't have to set this bit if it is already set in the module flags word. NOTE: this is not implemented in Twilight II v2.

Message 3: LoadSetupT2

`LoadSetupT2` tells your module to load any configuration or data resources. Remember that you are loading resources under someone else's memory ID, so be sure to `DetachResource` your resources immediately after `LoadResource`, and then to `SetHandleID` your detached resources to `T2Data2` (hi) so that they will stay around long enough for you to use them in your `BlankT2` handler. (Alternatively, you may also save the existing resource application, `ResourceStartup` (`MMStartUp`), load your resources, `ResourceShutDown`, and restore the old resource application. You still must detach your resources, but you don't have to bother with `SetHandleID`.)

Twilight II sets up the resource search path so that Twilight. Setup is on top. If you currently need to load data resources contained in your own resource fork, do an `LGetPathname2` to find out your pathname (use fileNum = $0001), and open (and close) your resource fork when appropriate by yourself. Be sure to save and restore the previous current resource file. C code that does this follows. ID is your module's memory ID, as returned from `MMStartUp`.

```
word MyResFile, OldResFile;

OldResFile=GetCurResourceFile();
MyResFile=OpenResourceFile(1 /* read only*/, NULL,
LGetPathname2(ID, 0x0001));
CloseResourceFile(MyResFile);
SetCurResourceFile(OldResFile);
```

In most cases, all resources should be loaded at this time! This includes both configuration resources of yours in the `Twilight. Setup` file, and static (unchanging) data resources of yours in your own resource fork. If your module has sound effects, then it would be a good idea to store them as `rSound` resources and also load them at this time. Keep track of your allocated memory handles yourself – be sure to dispose of them in the `UnloadSetupT2` handler. It is guaranteed that after `LoadSetupT2` is called, your module will remain in memory, in the same location, through the time `UnloadSetupT2` is called.

Please see the special section "Special Notes on When Resources Are and Should Be Loaded" under "Setup Resources" for when `LoadSetupT2` will get called, and if you should indeed load all your data resources (from your own resource fork) during it, or if your module qualifies as a special case that should load data resources during `BlankT2`. It probably doesn't, but read and be sure.

`T2Message`   =   `LoadSetupT2` ($0003.)

`T2Data1`   =   Reserved (do *not* modify!)

`T2Data2` (hi)   =   Reserved (do *not* modify!)

`T2Data2` (lo)   =   Flag word. Presently only bit 0 is defined (lmi = load message input):

`lmiOverrideSound $0001`
1 = override sound, 0 = sound okay. If sound is overridden, you should not load any of your sounds into memory (to conserve memory.)

`T2Result`   =   Bits defined as follows (lmr = load message result):

`lmrReqUsableScreen    $0001`
Requires usable screen after all. You don't have to set this bit if it is already set in your module flags word.

`lmrFadeOut  $0002`
Fade out after all. You don't have to set this bit if it is already set in your module flags word.

`lmrMostCommonPalette    $0004`
Do most common palette (mcp) after all. You don't have to set this bit if it's already set in your module flags word.

`lmrPrematureExit $0008`

While not implemented in Twilight II v2, this bit is very important and you must support it. This bit must be set if your module plans to exit before movePtr becomes true. For instance, Mountains, Plasma, String Art, etc. should set this bit only when their "Quit After One" option is selected. You don't have to set this bit if it's already set in your module flags word (as it is for modules like Short Out and Color by Color, which always exit early in random mode.)

Message 4: UnloadSetupT2

UnloadSetupT2 gives you the chance to dispose of any old memory handles that you previously had in memory for the entire time your module was selected. When you receive an UnloadSetupT2 message, your module is about to be unloaded and disposed of, so make sure you don't leave any handles behind!

The resource search path is undefined.

T2Message	=	UnloadSetupT2 ($0004.)
T2Data1	=	Reserved (do *not* modify!)
T2Data2 (hi)	=	Reserved (do *not* modify!)
T2Data2 (lo)	=	Reserved (do *not* modify!)
T2Result	=	Reserved (do *not* modify!)

Message 5: KillT2

KillT2 gives you the chance to dispose of any memory handles that you previously had in memory during the time your module was being configured by the user. When you receive a KillT2 message, your module is about to be unloaded and disposed of, so make sure you don't leave any handles behind!

The resource search path will be set to: «Your Module», Twilight. Setup,Twilight.II,ControlPanel,Sys.Resources.

T2Message	=	KillT2 ($0005.)
T2Data1	=	Reserved (do *not* modify!)
T2Data2	=	Reserved (do *not* modify!)
T2Result	=	Reserved (do *not* modify!)

Message 6: HitT2

HitT2 gives you the chance to react immediately when the user clicks in any one of the controls in the setup window. It also gives *Twilight II* the chance to enable the save button.

T2Message	=	HitT2 ($0006.)
T2Data1	=	Handle to control in question.
T2Data2	=	ID of the control.
T2Result (hi)	=	Reserved (must currently return $0000.)
T2Result (lo)	=	Boolean result value indicating if save control should be enabled based on the control hit.

Setup Resources

Twilight II also features a new way of saving module preferences. Each module can have its own custom preferences and the preferences from all modules can all exist simultaneously! In addition, the new preference manager was fully designed with multi-user AppleShare networks in mind as well. Preferences are now stored in `Twilight.Setup`, saved in the modules folder which exists in the same directory as the CDev when the CDev runs its `BootCDev` message handler.

Twilight II first checks for the `Twilight.Setup` file on boot. If the setup file can't be found, it is created and initialized with some default resource values.

Storage

Predefined resource type assignment for Twilight.Setup file:

Resource Type	Description
`rT2ExtSetup1 ($1001)`	Reserved for internal CDev use. (Internal integer flags.)
`rT2ModuleWord ($1002)`	Available for any word-sized setup resources. (Unsigned word.)
`rT2String ($1010)`	Reserved to save pathnames of currently selected modules. (Pseudo-WStrings.)
`rByteArray ($1012)`	Available for any size setup resources. (unsigned char array.)

If your module supports user-configurable setup (as defined by the `fSetup` bit of the `T2ModuleFlags` word) then it must store the user's currently selected module options in the `Twilight.Setup` file at the appropriate time. All custom resource types other than those above are reserved. All existing resource IDs are also reserved.

This means that your module may use any resource IDs in any of the above resource types or any of the Apple defined resource types that is not already taken when your module receives a `SaveT2` message. If your module needs to store information that is suited by a predefined Apple resource type, then use the Apple type. For instance, YouDrawit! and Movie Theater store the pathname of their currently selected files as `rWString` resources. If your module needs to store any word-sized configuration resources, then please use the `rT2ModuleFlags` resource type. If none of the above resource types or the Apple defined resource types suits your use, then please contact us with your ideas and we may assign a new custom resource type that all modules will be able to take advantage of in a future version. It is imperative that you use resource names to keep track of your configuration resources.

Load and save them by name, not by ID! When creating a new resource from scratch, use `UniqueResourceID` and then `SetResourceName`. The new resource name System 6 Resource Manager calls make this pretty easy.

When Resources Are and Should Be Loaded

LoadSetupT2 is not always called on boot, and `UnloadSetupT2` is not always called right before your module is about to be shut down and disposed. The new logic governing when each of these messages is called depends on whether the boot disk is a SCSI hard disk or not. If the boot disk is not a SCSI hard disk, `LoadSetupT2` will be called during boot, and `UnloadSetupT2` will be called only before your module is about to be shut down and disposed (i.e. when *Twilight II* has been purged, or when the user has selected a new module.)

If the boot disk is a SCSI hard disk, `LoadSetupT2` will be called when it is time to blank, right before calling `BlankT2`, and `UnloadSetupT2` will be called right after your `BlankT2` routine. This has the advantage of saving precious memory, while still making users without hard drives pretty happy. However, there are cases where this logic doesn't work the best it could. For these cases, two new bits of `T2ModuleFlags` have been defined: `fLoadSetupBoot`, and `fLoadSetupBlank`. You should use these bits in the situation where you think the internal logic described above isn't best for your module. For instance, the Tiler module only needs to load six bytes of configuration resources. Since this is very minimal, it keeps them in memory all the time the module is loaded, by setting fLoadSetupBoot. The YouDrawit module, on the other hand, loads the active animation template file in LoadSetupT2. This file can use anywhere from $7D00 to $9A00 bytes of memory, so it is not wise to make it stay in memory all the time under any situation. As such, the file is only loaded right before blanking, by setting fLoadSetupBlank.

It should be noted that when your module is called as a result of the user clicking the "blank now" button, *Twilight II* forces your setup to be called at blank (obviously.)

Likewise, there also are cases where it may be unwise for your module to load all its data resources from its resource fork at LoadSetupT2 time. Say, for instance, you have a module that displays a random rPString from your resource fork. And say you have 1000 pString resources in your resource fork, but only several random ones will be used each time your module is called. It would be a waste to load in all 1000 when you're only going to use several random ones that change each time your module is called. In rare cases like this, I suggest you load the few resources you need in your BlankT2 handler (and dispose of them before returning.)

This process is not encouraged except in rare cases like the one above. For this reason, *Twilight II* does not have things all nice and spiffy for you to load your resources at BlankT2 time. You must do all the dirty work. This isn't too much of a big deal - all you really have to do is:

```
OldRezFile = GetCurResourceFile
ResourceStartup (MyID)
RezFileID = OpenResourceFile (LGetPathname2)
load your resources...
blank your stuff until MovePtr = TRUE...
release/dispose your resources...
CloseResourceFile (RezFileID)
ResourceShutDown
SetCurResourceFile (oldFile)
return to Twilight II.
```

Miscellaneous Notes

Using Sound in Modules

Several guidelines have been established for modules using digitized sound effects played through the Apple IIGS's Ensoniq sound chip. By following these, sound can be implemented with a minimal amount of effort, and in a consistent fashion that the user can control and understand. The following points comprise the first recommended way for using sound effects:

1. Make sure you have an option allowing the user to turn the sound effects off. This is important, even if your module has no other setup options. Preferably this option should allow the user to change the sound volume as well. For instance, have a control where the volume can be changed from 0 to 15. At zero, there are no sound effects. Users want a feature like this!

2. Note the newly defined **T2Data2** (lo) flag word passed to your module at **LoadSetupT2** time. If bit 0 of this flag is on, then you also should not play any sound effects. This is the global sound shutoff Boolean flag, and you must honor it.

3. Keep your sounds stored as **rSound** resources. These can be loaded and detached at **LoadSetupT2** time and disposed of at **UnloadSetupT2**. If the user has requested not to have sound effects, or if the global sound shutoff flag is true, then you should not waste memory with loading in your sound resources from disk. You might want to consider allowing use of **rSound** resources in the Sounds folder, but that currently involves a lot of extra coding work!

4. You can use Apple's Sound control panel to play sounds. In C:

   ```
   SendRequest(6 /* srqPlaySoundSample */,
   stopAfterOne, NULL, TheRSound.Handle, NULL);
   ```

   If you need to play several sounds at once or require greater flexibility than the above method offers, you may play the sounds yourself using the Sound Manager. *Twilight II* has several requests that make this easier for you.

When calling *Twilight II*, send your request to "DYA~Twilight II~". We also have sample source code available that illustrates this method. Three *Twilight II* IPC requests were designed for sound:

$9005-t2StartupTools

If any errors occur during startup, no tools will be started and no memory will be allocated.

dataIn (lo)   Integer bit flags specifying which tools to start up. The following bits currently defined in Twilight II v 1.1 ($0110):
> bit 0 = start SANE
> bit 1 = start Sound Manager

dataIn (hi)   Word UserID to allocate tool direct page memory with.

dataOut   Pointer to the following 4-byte structure:
> +00 (word) = receive count (used by Tool Locator)
> +02 (word) = any errors incurred in the startup

$9006-t2ShutdownTools

Any tools started by **t2StartupTools** should be shutdown by this procedure. Their direct page memory will also be disposed.

dataIn (lo)   Integer bit flags specifying which tools to shut down. The following bits currently defined in Twilight II v 1.1 ($0110):
> bit 0 = shutdown SANE
> bit 1 = shutdown Sound Manager

dataIn (hi)   Reserved (Pass zero)

dataOut   Reserved.

$900D-t2CalcFreqOffset

This request will take a `relPitch` value from an `rSound` header and convert it into a corresponding `freqOffset` to be used with the Sound Manager.

dataIn (lo)   `relPitch` value from `rSound` header.
dataIn (hi)   Reserved (Pass zero).
dataOut   Pointer to the following 4-byte structure:
            +00 (word) = received count (used by Tool Locator)
            +02 (word) = `freqOffset`

These three requests should make handling your own sound effects with the Sound Manager much easier. Just remember to not use sound if the Sound Manager is already in use when you gain control!

Using Fonts in Modules

Twilight II now starts up the Font Manager before calling `BlankT2`. This means it is okay for your module to make Font Manager calls such as `InstallFont` and `SetPurgeStat`. However, you should be aware that some users may not have their system disk online at all times, and if you call `InstallFont` with the boot disk offline, the Font Manager will probably not be very complying. Be sure to react accordingly. In the future, *Twilight II* may start up the Font Manager at `LoadSetupT2` and `UnloadSetupT2` time to be more friendly to users with limited volumes, but at this time such action is not supported.

"Usable" Screens

A usable screen is defined as a screen which contains enough content to make it worth modifying by another module. For instance, Tiler leaves the screen in a state which Color by Color can work with. Short Out does not leave a usable screen, so if the screen is shorted out (to black) and another module is run directly afterward that requires a usable screen (like Tiler), then *Twilight II* will restore the screen before running Tiler.

If your module always requires or always leaves a usable screen, set the appropriate bit in the module flag word. If your module only sometimes requires or leaves a usable screen (such as snow, due to the clear screen option), then you can return this information at LoadSetupT2 and/or BlankT2 time.

We request that you follow the above guidelines so Random Mode can be enhanced now and even more in the future.

Low Memory Mode

Low memory mode saves users 32k of memory. LMM affects one situation: when $012000-A000 has been allocated (in a handle exactly $8000 bytes in size) but SHR shadowing is off when it is time to blank the screen. *Twilight II* will not allocate shadowing in this situation if LMM is on, because both banks $01 and $E1 of SHR must be preserved.

"Quit After One":
When You Need It and How to Implement It

Some modules (e.g. Mountains, Plasma, String Art, Headlines, etc.) have options to quit to the next module in random mode after they have generated a one screen display. This type of option is to tie users over until a definite "In Random Mode, Exchange Modules After X Minutes" is implemented for the future.

If you would like to implement this option, make sure you set the appropriate usable screen bits for your modules. Then code your module like this:

1. Call t2GetInfo (request $9004 to "DYA~Twilight II~", stopAfterOnei+sendToName) around the start of your module's BlankT2 message to find the count_selected_modules word. Use a dataIn of NIL and a dataOut such as the following. (You also can the dataOut supplied in our T2.H header file, but this one here is more efficient for reading only this one word.)

```
Word recvCount;
Word start offset = $0002;    /* copy from this byte of the
                                buffer */
Word end offset = $0004;      /* to this byte of the buffer */
Word count_selected_modules; /* t of selected modules */
```

2. When you think you should return to T2 to quit to the next module,
   you may only return with `bmrNextModule` in `T2Result` if
   `bmiBlankNow` (passed as an input at `BlankT2` time) is clear and
   `count_selected_modules` is equal to more than one.

Restoring or Saving the Original Screen

Twilight II has (obviously) saved the contents of the screen
before your module was run. What if your module needs to restore
the original screen? Or what if your module needs to reference the
original screen? For instance, Meltdown takes the original screen
and reverses it after a few minutes; a few minutes later it restores the
original screen back. Dissolve needs a copy of the original screen to
reference in order to do its effect. In these cases, you can make the
Twilight II `t2GetBuffers` IPC request ($900B).

You may *not* dispose of the handles this call returns, nor may you
modify the pixel data! Ignore the auxiliary buffer handle (which is
normally not used), and the palette buffer handle (which is used only
for background blanking.) Also, please note that this call returns
the original screen. The original screen is not necessarily what was
on screen before your module was called! For instance, in random
mode, your module can be called after another one. Thus, on screen
is the previous module's display and in the buffer is the original user's
screen. React and plan accordingly.

Here is C source code defining the structure returned by
`t2GetBuffers`. `DataOut` should be set to a pointer to this structure.
`DataIn` should be set to NIL.

```
#define t2GetBuffers        0x900Bu

/* DataOut structure for t2GetBuffers */
typedef struct getBuffersOut {
    Word recvCount;
    void ** shr_main_bufferH;    /* handle to main SHR buffer */
    void ** shr_aux_bufferH;     /* handle to aux SHR buffer */
    void ** palette_bufferH;     /* handle to palette buffer */
};
```

APPENDIX IV

IPC MODULE COMMANDS

The following IPC commands are available to your modules. Send your requests to: `DYA~Twilight II~`

$8000 - reqOpenT2PrefFile

Open the T2 preference file (currently "Twilight.Setup"). If it doesn't exist, create it. Return ID of the rezFile if opened successfully, else return error code.

dataIn: NIL.

dataOut: Requires two word fields

@+02 (word) Resource file ID of preferences resource file. (From OpenResFile)

@+04 (word) Error code, if any errors occurred. Zero if no errors.

$8001 - reqFadeOut

Fade the SHR screen out (modifying bank $e1 palettes).

dataIn: NIL.
dataOut: NIL.

$8002 - reqFadeIn

Fade the SHR screen in (modifying bank $e1 palettes)

dataIn: Pointer to $200 bytes of destination palettes.
dataOut: NIL.

$8003 - reqBlankScreen

Requests to blank the screen.

dataIn: Pointer to special structure:

+00 blankNowFlag: boolean -

   IF TRUE, we are being called from the "blank now" control:
     = do NOT call SysBeep2 for screen is blanking/unblanking
     = DO _force_ setup to be loaded and unloaded
     = DO pass a flag to the module telling it we're calling it like this

   IF FALSE, we are being called from the init:
     = DO call SysBeep2 for screen is blanking/unblanking
     = do NOT _force_ setup to be loaded and unloaded
     = DO pass a flag to the module telling it we're calling it like this

+02 moduleMemID: word   - memory ID to pass to module

+04 T2moduleFlags: word   - t2moduleflags for module

+06 moduleEntryPt: long   - JML MODULE_START (h'5c', i3'module_start')

+0A prefRezFileID: word   - resource file ID of opened pref resource file
                       only used if preffile is already open

+0C prefRezAppID: word   - resource application id pref rezfile opened
                     previously under
                     IF ZERO then the rezApp won't be set (only the
                     currfile will be when preffile is already open)

+0E LSResult: long   - result from loadsetupt2 of module
                  or NIL if setup hasn't been loaded yet.

+12 size

prefRezFileID and prefRezAppID are not needed if the prefFile is not already open.

dataOut: Undefined.

96

$8004 - `reqLoadModule`

Loads a module into memory. An old module MUST have already been unloaded, and UnloadSetupT2 called, if necessary.

dataIn: Handle to module pathname.

dataOut: Pointer to following structure:

>   +00 (word) - receive count
>   +02 (word) - errors (0 if none)
>   +04 eos - end of structure

$8005 - `reqInstallNDA`

Install the Twilight II NDA.

dataIn: Undefined.

dataOut: Undefined.

$8006 - `reqRemoveNDA`

Requests to remove the NDA.

dataIn: Undefined.

dataOut: Undefined.

$8007 - reqDLZSS

Unpacks a memory area.

dataIn:

+00 (word) - eor value
+02 (long) - input pointer - bit 15 set means that T2 will check MovePtr
+06 (long) - output pointer
+10 (long) - output length
+14 eos IF bit 15 clear above ELSE
+14 (word) - true if dlzss exited because of movePtr becoming true
+16 eos

dataOut: Undefined.

$8008 - reqConcatenate

Combine 2 pathnames, the former a folder and the latter a filename. Adjust the number of delimiters and everything.

dataIn:

Pointer to special structure

+00 (long) - folderpathptr - GS/OS C1InputString of folder pathname
+04 (long) - filenameptr - GS/OS C1InputString of filename
+08 (word) - memoryid - memory id to use to allocate new path handle
+0A eos

A filename can't have a leading delimiter – you've been warned!

dataOut:

Pointer to the following structure:

+00 (word) count - count
+02 (long) newpathnamehandle - handle of new path name created

$8009 - reqRandomize

Pick a new random module and make it current while this does not
check if random mode is on or off, if there is only one saved pathname,
it will always use it.

dataIn: Reserved.

dataOut: Pointer to following structure:

> +00 (word) - receive count
> +02 (word) - errors (0 if none)
> +04 - eos - end of structure

$800A - reqRemoveT2

Remove most traces of *Twilight II* from the system.

dataIn: Reserved.

dataOut: Reserved.

$800B - reqSetBuffers

Sets the SHR buffers.

dataIn: Pointer to structure

> +00 (long) - handle to E1 buffer ($8000 bytes). -1= use
> existing (no change)
>
> +04 (long) - handle to 01 buffer ($8000 bytes). -1= use
> existing (no change)
>
> +08 - eos - end of structure

dataOut: Reserved.

$9000 - t2TurnOn

Turn T2 on. This is ALMOST the equivalent of pressing shift-clear to turn T2 back on.

dataIn: Reserved.
dataOut: Reserved.

$9001 - t2TurnOff

Turn T2 off. This is ALMOST the equivalent of pressing shift-clear to turn T2 back off.

dataIn: Reserved.
dataOut: Reserved.

$9002 - t2BoxOverrideOff

Turn blinking box on by turning the override flag off. This is the temporary (i.e. not saved to disk) equivalent of turning on the blinking box checkbox in Setup: Options. The box will only be turned on if the user has the box turned on in setup. In other words, the override flag will be ignored if the box is already turned off in setup.

dataIn: Reserved.
dataOut: Reserved.

$9003 - t2BoxOverrideOn

Turn blinking box off by turning on the box override flag. This is the temporary (i.e. not saved to disk) equivalent of turning off the blinking box checkbox in Setup: Options. The box will only be turned off if the user has the box turned off in setup. In other words, the override flag will be ignored if the box is already turned off in setup.

dataIn: Reserved.
dataOut: Reserved.

$9004 - t2GetInfo

Return the state of/information on several aspects of *Twilight II*.

dataIn: reserved (pass zero)

dataOut:

Pointer to the following structure

+0 (word output) - count

+2 (word input) - start buffer offset (from this byte)

+4 (word input) - end buffer offset (to this byte). The end buffer offset
                  minus start buffer offset = SIZE

+6 (byte array output) - returned information output buffer
                         where +06 + SIZE - eos - end of structure

Buffer information available (`-`=through)

+0 (word) - state word
+2 (word) - number of modules selected in random mode (1 if rm off)
+4 (word) - version of Twilight II
+6 (long) - pointer to 320 mode don't blank cursor
+A (long) pointer to 640 mode don't blank cursor

The state word structure currently defined bits as follows:

bit 0 - current blinking box setup status
        - %0 = blinking box turned off in setup
        - %1 = blinking box turned on in setup

bit 1 - current blinking box override status
        - %0 = blinking box override off
        - %1 = blinking box override on

bit 2 - current background blank state
        - %0 = screen is not currently background blanked
        - %1 = screen is currently background blanked

bit 3 - current foreground blank state
- %0 = screen is not currently foreground blanked
- %1 = screen is currently foreground blanked

bit 4 - current active status - i.e. shift-clear
- %0 = twilight currently on
- %1 = twilight currently off

bit 5 - random mode on/off
- %0 = random mode off
- %1 = random mode on

$9005 - t2StartupTools

If any errors occur during startup, no tools will be started and no memory will be allocated.

dataIn (lo):

Integer bit flags specifying which tools to start up. The following bits currently defined in Twilight II v1.1 ($0110):

bit 0 - start SANE
bit 1 - start Sound Manager

dataIn (hi):

Word UserID to allocate tool direct page memory with.

dataOut:

Pointer to the following 4-byte structure:

+0 (word) - receive count (used by Tool Locator)
+2 (word) - any errors incurred in the startup

$9006 - t2ShutdownTools

Any tools started by t2StartupTools should be shutdown by this procedure. Their direct page memory will also be disposed.

dataIn(lo):

Integer bit flags specifying which tools to shut down. The following bits currently defined in Twilight II v1.1 ($0110):

bit 0 - shutdown SANE
bit 1 - shutdown Sound Manager

dataIn (hi) dataOut: Reserved (Pass zero).

dataOut: Reserved.

$9007 - t2ShareMemory

This is an area of memory that can be used by your module.

dataIn: Reserved.

dataOut: Pointer to structure:

        +0 (word) - count
        +2 (word) - size of buffer
        +4 (long) - pointer to buffer

You may modify this buffer at your leisure; it's not going anywhere. However, you _must_ get its address each time you receive MakeT2 or BlankT2 or whatever.. don't assume that it won't move (because if purge is pressed, it _will_ move!

It is suggested that you use the first two bytes of this 16 byte buffer as an ID word. Stick a unique integer value in it so you know if someone else overwrote your buffer!

$9008 - t2SetBlinkProc

Set a custom procedure called to blink the *Twilight II* menubar box.

dataIn: Pointer to custom blink procedure. If 0, the current procedure is removed

dataOut: Reserved.

The custom blink procedure will be called every half a second or so almost without fail. It will be called even if the user has the normal blinking box turned off in setup, so if you wish to honor the user's request of not to blink, call T2GetCurState and look at bit 0. In most cases, I would think that you would want to honor the user's wish not to blink the box, but I leave it at the discretion of the programmer.

In addition to JSL'ing to your custom handler the normal box will STILL blink the normal box, so be sure to set the override flag if you don't wish this to happen!

Only applications may make this call. Keep your routine VERY SMALL; I suggest you only set a flag or something similar.

$9009 - t2ForceBkgBlank

Force [SHR] background blank, when the delay has elapsed.

dataIn: bit 0 is significant
            - %0 = stop forcing
            - %1 = start forcing

dataOut: Reserved.

$900A - t2BkgBlankNow

Force a background blank, NOW!

dataIn: Reserved.

dataOut: Reserved.

Currently, this will only work in SHR desktop programs. You can't force a text bkg blank. This might change in the future.

$900B - t2GetBuffers

Return handles to the two 32k SHR memory buffers, and a palette buffer.

dataIn: Reserved.

dataOut: Pointer to the following structure

+0 (word) - count

+2 (long) - handle to E1 buffer ($8000 bytes).

+6 (long) - handle to 01 buffer ($8000 bytes) or NIL if none.

+10 (long) - handle to palette buffer ($200 bytes).

+14 - eos - end of structure

$900C - t2Reserved1 (was t2GetVersion)

Not implemented.

$900D - t2CalcFreqOffset

This request will take a relPitch value from an rSound header and convert it into a corresponding freqOffset to be used with the Sound Manager.

dataIn (lo): relPitch value from rSound header.

dataIn (hi): Reserved (Pass zero).

dataOut: Pointer to the following 4-byte structure:
+00 (word) = received count (used by Tool Locator)
+02 (word) = freqOffset

$9020 - t2PrivGetProcs (private IPC call)

Return pointers to confidential *Twilight II* routines. The available pointer list is the following:

```
1: 00-03 = set_random_seed
2: 04-07 = random
3: 08-0B = setup_plot
4: 0C-0F = get_pixel
5: 10-13 = set_pixel
6: 14-17 = getset_pixel
```

dataIn (lo): End byte offset (see above) - must be multiple of 4!

dataIn (hi): Start byte offset (see above) - must be multiple of 4!

dataOut: Pointer to the following structure

+0 (word) - count
+2 (long) - [x numLongs]
+6 (long) - [example]
+A (long) - [example]
+2+NumLongs*4 - eos - end of structure

Conclusion

Well, that wasn't so bad, was it? The format is quite complex, but after you've dealt with it for a bit, it makes much more sense. Be sure to make full use of the sample source code we provide – it can help a lot! Your feedback is also welcome for extensions and modifications to the format.

INDEX

- D -

- E -

- I -

- L -

- M -

- O -

- P -

- R -

- S -

- T -

- W -